Political Economy of Bodo Movement

A Human Development Perspective

Political Economy of Bodo Movement

A Human Development Perspective

Dr. Keshab Basumatary

AKANSHA PUBLISHING HOUSE
NEW DELHI • GUWAHATI • VISAKHAPATNAM

AKANSHA PUBLISHING HOUSE
4649-B/21, Ansari Road
Darya Ganj, New Delhi - 110 002
Ph.: 23263193 / 9811582579 / 09435116718
Fax: 011-23263193
Email: ektabooks@yahoo.com
www.akanshapublishinghouse.com

Political Economy of Bodo Movement:

First Published 2012
ISBN 978-81-8370-321-5

PRINTED IN INDIA

Published by Akansha Publishing House, New Delhi and Printed at Harmain Offset, Delhi.

Dedicated

To

My Mother and Father

Contents

Foreword

The new development paradigm, evolved in last few decades, has shifted the attention away from the commodity-centered approach of per capita income to people-centric discourse of development thinking. The notion is simply to put people of all spheres in the forefront of all socio-economic and ethno-political activities that take place around us. This development paradigm recognizes the feelings and expectations of the people to live their lives according to their choices, and simultaneously, the importance to respect the aspirations of others. The broadest possible definition of development – *expansion of freedom* compels the policy makers across the globe to recast their age-old development strategies. The concept of well-being under the aegis of human development approach identifies the non-economic events that cause capability deprivation at individual level, and their many-faced consequences often thwart achieving the ultimate goal of evolving an inclusive and sustainable developmental trajectory. In the backdrop of Bodo movement in Assam the present effort focuses a deeper look on the issue through the lens of human development. Identity, as recognized by the proponents of new development paradigm, plays a crucial role in human life, however, the broader outline of the same varies significantly over time and across situation. Dr. Basumatary applies clear theoretical sense of development economics in his present assessment of progress of an ancient ethnic group living in Assam, but upholds the perception of common people to define and describe development. This book, I am sure, will contribute significantly to the existing literature of human development.

Dr. Santanu Ray
Department of Planning & Statistical Cell
North-Eastern-Hill University (NEHU)
Shillong-793022

Preface

It is pertinent to note that this study is an attempt to capture the real picture on Bodo Movement through human development perspective. This study has been organized into seven chapters. After the introductory chapter which summarizes identity issues in modern development discourse, presents the historical background of Bodo Movement in Assam and seeks to view the movement through the lenses of human development. Chapter second reviews the existing literature on Bodo community and their movement to capture a holistic profile of the political economy of the region. It covers a wide-ranging issues related to their socioeconomic conditions, linguistic and cultural heritage, ethnic aspects, political developments and a brief history of Bodo aspirations in pre- and post-Independence era. Chapter three draws the framework designed to carry out the present research study. It narrates the objectives of the study, sets the hypotheses, and discusses the methodology adopted to fulfill the objectives. This chapter also introduces the nature and sources of data used in this study to test the hypothesis.

Taking the stock of secondary information Chapter four intends to evaluate the status of human development of Bodo inhabited districts of Assam as compared to other districts. The purpose of this chapter is to present a comparative analysis of development indicators. First, identity of Bodos has been very briefly introduced and looked at the demographic profile of the state in such a fashion that the Bodo dominated settlements could be spotted. This section also discusses the population characteristics as well as the demographic transition that had taken place in the state during 1990s. Next, captures the socioeconomic profile of these districts as compared to the state as a whole and finally summarized the status of human development in the state with special reference to Bodo-inhabited districts.

Chapter fifth deals with primary data to enumerate the status of human development of Bodo population living in the rural areas of Bodoland Territorial Area Districts (BTAD). Adopting the similar methodology of Human Development Report Assam (2003), this chapter constructs the Human Development Index for each of the sample villages. Adjusting them for sample errors Human Development Indices for all the four districts under BTAD as well as for the Bodos living in the areas under BTAD are obtained by applying standard statistical tools.

Chapter six intends to capture the dynamics of Bodo aspiration on development and long-lasting movement through *Focus Group Discussions* (FGD). This chapter is based on the qualitative judgments of the respondents on the priorities and their understanding of well-beings, and thereby, capabilities. Chapter seven decides about the hypotheses, set in Chapter three on the basis of the findings in Chapter four, five & six, and derives some policy recommendations.

Finally presents the references at the end of the work. This book is based on my research work carried out at North Eastern Hill University, Shillong, Meghalaya and UGC has provided me two years study leave through faculty improvement programme under 11th plan period. I therefore express my profound gratitude to the UGC and the staff.

I express my heartfelt gratitude to my Supervisor Prof. P. Nayak, for all the valuable time and effort that he has provided in supervising this work. He has not only provided his able guidance to complete my work in time, but also has taught me the finer details of economic analysis. I remain always indebted to him. I am also thankful to all the faculty members and the office staff of the Department of Economics, NEHU, for their words of encouragement and moral support during the course of my research work.

I also owe my special gratitude to Dr. Santanu Ray and his colleagues in Statistical Cell, NEHU for providing me the necessary technical help in analysing the data.

I am personally thankful to Dr. P.C. Nag, Principal, B.B. Kishan College, Jalah for sparing his valuable time and for extending all the supports in completing this research work. In this context, I acknowledge my indebtedness to my colleagues in the college for their moral support and inspiration.

My special thanks are also due to Dr Jugal Saikia, Shri Chittaranjan Musahary, Shri Sankhang Basumatary, Shri Suneel Basumatary, and my beloved Garpa for their generous help in different stages of this research work.

I am really grateful to my wife Sewali, my son Devid and daughter Farina for their encouragements and facilitating congenial environment at home in connection with this work.

Last but not the least, I recall the tremendous efforts of both my mother and brother which made me able to reach at this stage of my life besides my publishers who transformed this endeavour into reality.

Baksa
May 2012

Keshab Basumatary

List of Tables

List of Figures

List of Maps

Abbreviations

AAMSU	All Assam Minority Students Union
AASU	All Assam Students Union
AAPTL	All Assam Plains Tribal League
AATS	All Assam Tribal Sangha
ABEF	All Bodo Employees Federation
ABSU	All Bodo Students Union
ABWWF	All Bodo Women Welfare Federation
AGP	Assam Gana Parishad
AHDR	Assam Human Development Report
AQLR	Adult Literacy Rate (%)
ASDC	Autonomous State Demand Committee
BAC	Bodoland Autonomous Council
BFF	Bodo Farmers' Federation
BJP	Bharatiya Janata Party
BLT	Bodo Liberation Tigers
BPAC	Bodo Peoples Action Committee
BSF	Bodo Security Force
BSS	Bodo Sahitya Sabha
BTF	Bodo Teachers Forum
BVF	Bodo Volunteer Force
BTAD	Bodoland Territorial Area District

BTC	Bodoland Territorial Council
BWA	Bodo Writers Academy
CER	Combined Gross Enrolment Ratio (%)
GDP	Gross Domestic Product
GNP	Gross National Product
HD	Human Development
HDI	Human Development Index
HDR	Human Development Report
MHRD	Ministry of Human Resource Development
NDFB	National Democratic Front of Bodoland
NER	North Eastern Region
NIHDI	Non-Income Human Development Index
NSDP	Net State Domestic Product
PCGDP	Per Capita Gross Domestic Product
PCGSDP	Per Capita Gross State Domestic Product
PCNSDP	Per Capita Net State Domestic Product
PPP	Purchasing Power Parity
PQLI	Physical Quality of Life Index
PTCA	Plain Tribal Council of Assam
SDP	State Domestic Product
SHDR	State Human Development Report
TS	Tribal Sangha
UNDP	United Nations Development Program

1
Introduction

Identity Issues in Development Discourse

Capability approach focuses direct attention on identity issues. The Nobel Laureate Economist and Philosopher Amartya Sen used the ideas of social identity in 1970s while establishing the foundations of capability approach against the traditional concept of utilitarianism (Sen 1977, 1979). In his recent concerns with culture and public reasoning identity plays a critical role in articulating a wide range of issues closely linked with his capability approach (Sen 2005, 2006). The idea of social identity has been put forward in a research agenda centered on the notions of freedom, rationality, morality, culture and democracy (Comin and Teschl 2006). Development can be seen as a process of expanding the real freedoms that people enjoy. Focusing on human freedoms contrasts with narrow views of development such as identifying development with the growth of gross national product or with the rise in national incomes or with industrialization or with technological advance or with social modernization. Growth of gross national product or individual income of course very important as means to expanding the freedoms enjoyed by the members of the society. But the freedoms depend also on other determinants such as social and economic arrangement as of facilities for education and health as well as political and civil rights such as the liberty to participate in public discussion and scrutiny.

Similarly, industrialization as well as technological progress and social modernization can substantially contribute to expanding human freedom but freedom depends on other influences as well. If freedom is what development advances then there is a major argument for concentrating on that overarching objective rather than on some particular means or some specially chosen list of instruments. Viewing developments in terms of expanding substantive freedoms directs attention to the ends that make development important rather than merely to some of the means that play a prominent part in the process.

The capability approach emphasizes functional capabilities which are in fact a set of "substantive freedoms" such as the ability to live to old age, engagement in economic transactions, or participation in political activities. These are constructed in terms of the substantive freedoms people have reason to value, instead of utility or happiness, desire-fulfillment or choice or access to resources or income, commodities, and assets. Development requires the removal of major sources of unfreedom such as poverty, illiteracy and ill-health which are also understood as capability-deprivations. Poor economic opportunities as well as systematic social deprivation, neglect of public facilities as well as intolerance of repressive states. Despite unprecedented increases in overall opulence, the contemporary world denies basic freedoms to masses. Sometimes the lack of substantive freedoms relates directly to economic poverty which robs people of the freedom to satisfy hunger or to achieve sufficient nutrition as well as to obtain remedies for troublesome diseases or the opportunity to be adequately clothed or sheltered and to enjoy clean water or sanitation facilities. In other cases the unfreedom links closely to the lack of public facilities and social care such as the absence of organized arrangements for public health care and educational facilities and of the effective institutions for the maintenance of local peace and order. In still other cases the violation of freedom results directly from a denial of political and civil liberties by authoritarian regimes and from imposed restrictions on the freedom to participate in the social, political and economic life of the community. It is noteworthy that the emphasis is not only on how human beings actually function, but certainly on their capability outcome, which is a practical choice to function in important ways if they so wish. Someone could be deprived of such capabilities in many ways, e.g. by ignorance, government oppression, lack of financial resources, or false consciousness. This approach to human well-being emphasizes the importance of freedom of choice, individual heterogeneity and the multi-dimensional nature of welfare. The capability approach argues that the goal of any public policy and action is to enlarge a person's functioning and capacity to function or expand the range of activities that a person can efficiently perform (Sen, 2005). The capability of an individual, as defined in UNDP literature, includes the enabling opportunities given by schooling, health services etc. Additional choices include political freedom; religious freedom, environmental freedom, other guaranteed human rights and various ingredients of self respect.

The ultimate concern of today's development thinking is how to create an enabling environment where people of all spheres of life are capable enough to express their choices freely. Sen (1999) introduces the broadest possible definition of development – *expansion of freedoms*. His set of freedoms includes a wide range of human freedoms – freedom from hunger, illiteracy, disease; freedom from insecurity; from political, cultural and religious tyranny. They also include the positive freedoms of thought, cultural expression and the enjoyment of leisure and many of these issues are deeply associated with development and firmly rooted in day-to-day economic challenges of promoting sustainable and inclusive economic growth.

The history of human civilization witnessed worst conflicts on identity issues which often turned into violences. We have recently witnessed worst type of violence in Kosovo, Bosnia, Rwanda, Timor, Israel, Palestine, Sudan, and many other places in the world. Some of these conflicts permanently blur the very fabrics of human values. Therefore, the important and perhaps, most crucial task of our leaders have been to address the aspirations of the people with different identities, living in different federal units within the national boundary. The problem gets more acute when reasonable regional variations in socio-economic aspects and diversities in linguistic and cultural identities are parts of the national life. The feelings of dissatisfaction as well as of exclusion often become serious challenges for the national integrity and hamper the developmental activities. The worst sufferer of such disasters arising from the socio-political outburst and from following state action is primarily the weaker sections of the society- economically backward people, women and adolescents.

The strength of Indian democracy can easily be identified as apparent diversities in social, economic, religious and cultural life across the regions that work normally as unity. However, there are evidences of violence in different parts of the country in different occasions which could have been avoided by addressing the core of the issue in initial stages. The unnecessary delay in understanding the sentiments and aspirations of the people give fuel to the fire of dissatisfaction. The primary reason behind such unwanted happenings could be underdevelopment, exploitation, negligence, all of which are arising out either from poor governance or from non-governance.

Background of Bodo Movement in Assam

Ethnic Movement is a worldwide phenomenon. Ethnic conflict includes the conflict between the state and ethnic groups and inters ethnic conflicts. In India, ethnic conflicts or ethnicity based movements started in many parts of the country in early years of the twentieth century. There are evidences of such conflicts in north-eastern region of the country. In the context of the north-east India it is important to know as well as understand the societies and the social formations to come to grip with issues of ethnicity and the rising tide of identity movements among tribal as well as non-tribal communities. As is well known, consolidation of identities along the lines of tribe and community has become increasingly manifest in the recent years in this region. In recent decades there has been a total rethinking of the developmental strategies that have been adopted in the post-independence period. This rethinking has been partly stimulated by the still persisting socio-economic problems of both rural and urban masses as well as the neglected tribes of the regions.

The ethnic based movement or in other words, social bases which provide the resources of ethno-cultural mobilization among some of the north-eastern populations are examined here on the basis of three definable phases or periods such as pre-colonial, colonial and post-colonial or post-Independence periods. The ethnic movements in colonial India were born out of deep dissatisfaction and often discontent against socio-economic policies of the British Government which no doubt adversely affected their lives. The hills and plains of the region have been occupied by different streams of Mongoloid people who came from the north and the east at different periods well before the onset of colonial rule. It is generally agreed that the Mongoloids, mentioned as the *Kiratas* in ancient Sanskrit literature, once occupied practically the whole of the north-eastern region. The diverse Mongoloid groups which eventually settled in different habitats and ecological settings crystallized into distinct tribal societies. Even in the case of Assam plains, the early rulers were Indo-Mongoloids of various dynasties spanning a time period from fifth to mid-eleventh century. The local dynasties had contacts with Hindu states of India. While the hills and mountains of north-east India remained outside the orbit of Hindu influence and caste-based social formation, the history of Assam plains shows that by the twelfth century local kings of Mongoloid origin became Hindus. Then, there is the classic example of social transformation and subsequent contribution in shaping the regional society by the *Ahoms* who ruled over Assam for merely 600 years, from 1228 A.D. till the advent of the British in 1826. The *Ahom* period is of considerable significance where their rulers established a well-integrated administrative system in Assam and they also patronized the Hindu religious institutions. In pre-*Ahom* period, the social formations in Assam were predominantly tribal in nature. But through the development of a centralised power and state religion, the different ethnic groups were united and the Assamese as a wider social formation crystallized in the Brahmaputra plains. In this, the neo-*Vaishnava* religious movement under the leadership of Shankaradeva in the sixteenth century also played a significant role.

It is important to note that in the long centuries before the advent of British rule in the region, there was a high degree of fluidity in the socio-cultural arena so that intermingling of various streams of people, including biological admixture, produced diverse social alignments and group identities. The boundaries of the groups were never very rigid. It is this flexibility, characteristic of a frontier tract experiencing considerable population movement from different directions, which provided scope for shifting alliance and identities. Pre-colonial social setting in the region was more fluid and flexible than in the subsequent colonial and post-colonial periods. Thus, various 'tribal' inhabitants of the hills got integrated and often absorbed into the fold of the Hindu peasantry consequent on changing their niche from the hills to the plains. In the plains as Assam, tribal groups such as the *Bodo-Kachari*, *Rabha, Mech*, *Karbi* and the *Deuri-Chutiya* had thus, for centuries, provided the main source of Hindu population through a process of conversion and subsequent Sanskritization. The 'tribe' had never been a fixed or static category in those early times and there were many instances of change from tribal to non-tribal status. Contrary to popular notion, the numerous culturally and politically discrete communities of later times lived in a situation of contact and communication with their respective neighbouring populations. The conditions radically altered during a rather brief period (1826-1947) of British colonial rule. The annexation of Assam by the British (the East India Company) brought the people of this region into greater and deeper contact with sociopolitical currents then prevailing in the rest of the country. The channels of contact and the levels of communication were further accentuated in the early part of the 20th century. The British set in motion a series of moves in order to establish a degree of political and administrative dominance over the plains as well as the hill people. The British policies and the activities of Christian missionaries who came into the region contributed significantly in creating a freeze effect on the communities and social formations. Colonial rule and missionary activities also contributed significantly in detailing the character and tenor of identity movements among the tribal and non-tribal in the post-Independence period.

The impact of British administration became manifest through various means and measures such as the introduction of Inner Line Regulation in 1873 and the declaration of most of the hill areas as "Excluded Areas" under the provision of Government of India Act of 1935. Most tribal communities of the hills thus remained cut off from social and political developments taking place elsewhere. Mention must also be made of impressive population movements into the region during the British period unleashed by the imperatives of colonial administration and economy. In the context of an organized colonial economy with fairly strict monitoring of exploitable resources, coupled with immigration of diverse groups in a short period of time, the earlier resilience of the regional social system was lost forever. Each community tended to become a rigid social formation and this was to the utmost advantage of the colonial rulers. The accentuation of tribal-non-tribal differences and the formation of rigid social blocks out of indigenous castes and communities as well as recent migrants were important developments in the colonial period. Under the British rule, the administration of the tribal inhabited hills areas of the north eastern region, the then Assam was different from that prevailing in the rest of the country. In the period before India gained independence, the tribal areas of the north east India, were separated from the general administrative and constructional setup prevailing in the rest of the country. They were governed by a number of laws and one of these for instance; the Bengal Eastern Frontier Regulation of 1873 prohibited the entry of all non-hill tribal British subjects into the area within the Inner Line without a permit issued by the competent authority. The Inner Line Regulations ensured that the hill regions beyond the plains of Assam were largely left to their traditional chiefs once they accepted British suzerainty. The princely kingdoms of Tripura and Manipur were treated as dependencies, remote-controlled by political agents but not administered on a day-to-day basis. For the British, the Northeast remained a frontier, never a constituent region of the empire. Only Assam was integrated, its rich tea plantations and oilfields, its agricultural output and potential for industries providing enough justification for direct administrative control. As a result of these protective measures, the hill tribes were encouraged to distance themselves from the plainsmen and developed a special kind of identity that remained crucial for subsequent political events in the region (Das 1993).

There was long chronology of such resistance in north east region. In the last part of seventeen century the entire Jaintia tribe and the Garos rose against imposition of taxes and the Lushai-Kuki, Manipuri and many plains tribes in Assam raided British posts in the same century. The Birsa Munda movement at the beginning of nineteenth century too was directed against the outsiders namely landlords, traders and government officers. There was Naga resistance in seventeenth century and even an agrarian movement in 1893-94. The Sonaram (1902), Kuki (1917) movements (Singh 1982, Das, 1989) symbolized early ethnic struggles. Consequent upon the visit of the Statutory Commission in 1920s, further apprehension of marginalization, had grown among the tribal people and minority communities. Colonial rulers allowed missionary activities. Association with the Christian missionaries and gradual spread of education amongst the tribes and other communities infused a sense of self-esteem. This factor is crucial to understand the birth of ethno-nationalism eventually among the Nagas, Mizos, and the Manipuris. The Khasi, Ahom, Naga, Mizo, Bodo-Kachari, Miri and Deuri were the first to demand ethnic representation. The situation worsened further by the fact that famines in the latter half of the 19th Century forced the tribal into destitution. Elwin (1986) argues that the chief cause of the decline of tribal communities was the loss of land and forests which according to him had the effect of enervating tribal organism that it had no interior resistance against infection by a score of other evils.

Following Independence, the governmental approach to tribal was radically altered. The old policy of maintaining status quo and isolation was replaced by a policy of development and integration. The post-Independence period has been one of acceleration in the pace of social change and modernization of various tribal groups and their effective induction within the framework of the nation-state. However, it is also during the last five and a half decades since independence that the freeze effect in the various social formations became more vivid, functional and effective in turning tribes, castes, communities and language groups into ethnic blocks. Many groups have shown varying degrees of strain in accepting and adjusting to the demands of integration, which often has an assimilation overtone, made on them.

Thus, while the pre-colonial setting was fluid and flexible, the colonial and post-colonial settings have been less so and the societal boundaries became more rigid, doing in the process distinct cultural orientation—the phenomenon we call ethnicity. Societies became ethno-political blocks. In addition, this period is characterized by revivalist trend so that the various social formations looked to their primordial cultural assets to define and consolidate their boundaries. Ethnic self-consciousness and its consolidation and asserting along the lines of tribe, community or language groups have become increasingly manifest in the recent years in the entire region. In every one of the seven states that make up the north-eastern region, there is a comic perception of who constitute the 'insiders' and who are 'outsiders' vying for the limited number of jobs and other assets and resources of the respective territories. Regionalism along social and ethnic lines has been a dominant development in the years since Independence.

In the post-colonial north-east, we can recognise five different parameters of identity consolidation. These are tribe, caste, language, territory and religion. These often work in combination with one another. Emergence of tribal social formations, often with demand for specified territories as politico-administrative units are features common enough in north-east India these days. The context of smooth integration of tribal and non-tribal, of various language groups, of locals and immigrants and of various religious communities appear to be fraught with many hurdles. The consolidation of various social formations and ethnic upsurge based on it may be viewed as strategies of adaptation of the tribesmen and other indigenous inhabitants of the region in the modern context. The commotions that go with demand-making polities, including secessionist movements, have in the meantime, created unsettled conditions. But if we take a long-range view of history, we see that social unrest and mass stirrings have never been permanent attributes of human societies. These are like turning points in the life of a society, which is passing from one kind of articulation to another.

Before the advent of the British, no empire based in mainland India had controlled any part of what now makes up the country's northeast. Migration from the Indian mainland was limited to preachers and teachers, traders and soldiers of fortune. Mainland cultural influence was also limited to Assam, Manipur and Tripura, where the kings adopted variants of Hinduism as the state religion. The uninterrupted freedom from mainland conquest for a great length of history, coupled with the region's racial distinctiveness, gave its people a sense of being different from those in mainland India. So, India's northeast territories look less and less India and more and more like the highland societies of Southeast Asia. It is a polyglot region, its ethnic mosaic as diverse as the rest of the country. Of the 5,633 communities listed by the "People of India" project, 635 were categorized as tribal, of which 213 were found in the northeast India. This project also listed 325 languages of which 175 belonging to the Tibeto-Burman family found in northeast India. Some of the bigger Tribes, such as the Nagas, number around one million, the smallest, such as the Mates of Manipur have just a few thousand left. Even the bigger tribes are often mere generic identities rather than nationalities, without a common language (as in the case of the Nagas), held together more in opposition to the Indian nation-state than by an organic growth of national consciousness.

All of India's major religions are practiced here, with Christianity dominating the hills and Hinduism and Islam dominating the plains. Animistic faiths and Lamaist sects are also found in the region. Assamese and Bengali speakers are the most numerous but linguistic preferences in the region have often changed due to political considerations and have sometimes concealed ethnic and religious divisions. In Assam, the migrant Muslim peasantry of Bengali origin chose to register as Assamese speakers during every census after Independence to melt into the local milieu. The Assamese also co-opted Muslim migrants as Na-Asasimyas or neo-Assamese if only to ensure a predominant position of Assamese language in the state; in such situations linguistic predominance is what ethnic domination is often built on. But when these Muslims were targeted by the Assamese on a large scale during the 1983 riots, many of them started registering as Bengali speakers, leading to a decrease in the number of Assamese speakers in the subsequent decades.

In the pre-British era, the population flow into what is now northeast India almost wholly originated from the east. Being closer to the highlands of Burma and southwestern China than to the power centers of the Indian mainland, this region was exposed to a constant flow of tribes and nationalities belonging to the Tibeto-Burman stock, one settling down only to be overrun by the subsequent wave. The incomplete process of racial assimilation, the frequency of fresh migrations and the restrictive nature of empire building in the region account for its current ethnic diversity. But the direction of the population flow changed with the advent of the British. The colonial masters brought peasants and agricultural laborers, teachers and clerks from neighboring Bengal and Bihar to open up Assam's economy. The trickle became a tide, and the sweep was soon to cover states like Tripura, where the Manikya kings offered Bengali farmers "jungle-avadi" or forest clearance leases to popularize settled agriculture that would, in turn, increase the revenue. The hill regions were protected by the Inner Line Regulations; the plains and the Princely domains were not. The steady population flow from mainland India, particularly from undivided Bengal, accentuated the ethnic and religious diversity and introduced a nativist-outsider element to the simmering conflict. The Partition led to a rise in the flow of refugees and migrants from East Pakistan (now Bangladesh). Tripura's demography changed qualitatively in two decades, with the Bengalis becoming a clear majority. The pace of demographic change was slightly slower in Assam than in Tripura, but it was pronounced enough to upset the "sons of the soil," provoking both armed and unarmed protest movements. The fear that other northeastern states would "go the Tripura way" has weighed heavily on indigenous peoples and early settlers throughout the Northeast and provoked the more militant of them to take up arms. Subodh Debbarma, vice-president of the Tribal Students Federation (TSF) of Tripura, told a news conference in Guwahati, Assam, that "Assam would soon become another Tripura, where the sons of the soil have become aliens within half a century (Reported in *Sentinel* daily newspaper Guwahati, 3 June 2002).

A tradition of armed resistance to invaders developed in the region even before the British came. The Ahom kings fought back the Mughals, the Tripura kings fought back the Bengal sultans, but when the British went into the Northeast, they encountered fierce resistance in the Naga and the Mizo (then Lushai) hill regions in Manipur and in what is now

Meghalaya. The Naga and the Mizo tribesmen resorted to guerrilla war, holding up much stronger British forces by grit and ingenious use of the terrain until, in some places of the Mizo hills, entire villages were populated only by widows. After the British left, the Indian nation-state faced uprisings in Tripura almost immediately after Independence and in the Naga Hills since the mid-fifties. The Communists, who led the tribal uprising in Tripura, called off armed struggle in the early fifties and joined Indian-style electoral politics. But since the 1980 ethnic riots, Tripura has witnessed periodic bouts of tribal militancy, with the Bengali refugee population its main target. The Naga uprising, the strongest ethnic insurrection in northeast India has been weakened by repeated splits on tribal lines. Talks between the Indian government and the stronger faction of the National Socialist Council of Nagaland (NSCN), started in 1997, are continuing, but a possible resumption of Naga insurgency remains a worst-case scenario for Delhi in the Northeast. Armed uprisings erupted in the Mizo Hills following a famine in 1966. A year later, guerrilla bands became active in Manipur and Tripura. Since most of these rebel groups found safe bases, weapons and training in what was then East Pakistan, the defeat of the Pakistani armed forces in 1971 adversely affected the rebels from northeast India. For nearly seven years, they were deprived of a major staging post in a contiguous foreign nation. China, which trained and armed several batches of Naga, Mizo and Meitei since 1966, had stopped help by the early 1980s. By then, however, Bangladesh's military rulers, foisted to power by the bloody coup that killed the country's founder Sheikh Mujibur Rehman, had revived the Pakistani policy of sheltering, arming and training rebel groups from northeast India. Almost all the separatist groups in the Northeast Nagas, Mizos, Meiteis, Tripuris, and now even those from Meghalaya have subsequently received shelter and support in

Bangladesh. On the other hand, Indian agencies used the Northeast to arm and train, support and shelter the Bengali guerrillas against Pakistan in 1971 and then the tribal insurgents from Chittagong Hill Tracts against Bangladesh.

By the early 1980s, the whole region was gripped by large-scale violence. There were fierce riots in Tripura and Assam. Separatist movements intensified in Mizoram, Nagaland and Manipur, later spreading to both Assam and Tripura. India's young Prime Minister Rajiv Gandhi took the initiative to arrive at settlements with the militant students of Assam, the separatist Mizo National Front (MNF) and the Tribal National Volunteers of Tripura. But other insurgencies continued and new ones emerged. If the separatist movements such as those of the Nagas and the Mizos had challenged federal authority, the recent insurgencies of the Bodos, the Hmars, the Karbis and the Dimasa directly confront the regional power centers the new states of Northeast. If the Nagas and the Mizos fought for a separate country and finally settled for a separate state within India, the smaller ethnicities such as the Bodos or the Hmars fight for autonomous homelands they want carved out of the states such as Assam and Mizoram. Very often in the Northeast, a negotiated settlement with a separatist movement has opened the ethnic fissures within it. The Hmars, the Maras and the Lais fought shoulder to shoulder with the Lushai against the Indian security forces during the twenty years of insurgency led by the MNF. But twenty years of bonding through the shared experience of guerrilla warfare failed to develop a greater "Mizo" identity. The Bodos, the Karbis and the Dimasa all joined the Assam movement to expel "foreigners" and "infiltrators." But after settlements with the Indian government, they felt the Assamese "had taken the cake and left us the crumbs." The result: fresh agitations, often sliding into violent insurgencies, spearheaded by smaller ethnicities demanding separate homelands. The ethnic imbalance in power sharing has often caused retribalization, which has had its own cascading effect in restricting the growth of local nationalisms that could challenge the Indian state. After fighting India for forty years, Naga "nationalism" remains an incomplete process, its growth retarded by at least three major splits within the separatist movement, mostly along tribal lines.

The trend has been no different in Mizoram or Manipur. The Kuki demand for a separate homeland that pitted them against the Nagas has driven some smaller clans away from them and led to the emergence of a separate "Zomi" identity. Tribes such as the Paites prefer to be called "Zomis" and their militias have sided with the NSCN against the Kuki militant groups. The Hmars, Lais and the Maras have joined the Chakmas and the Reangs to challenge the Mizos. In Tripura, the Mizos in the northern Jampui hills demand a regional council within the Tribal Areas Autonomous Council of Tripura to preserve their "distinct identity," whereas their ethnic kinsmen in Mizoram are wary of similar demands by smaller ethnicities. The Reangs in Tripura resent attempts by the Tripuris to impose the Kok-borok language on them. And they look back at the brutal suppression of Reangs rebellions by the Tripuris kings as "evidence of ethnic domination that cannot be accepted anymore." These intra-tribal tensions have weakened efforts to promote a compact "Borok" or tribal identity against perceived Bengali domination. India's first prime minister, Jawaharlal Nehru, excluded the Northeast from the process of linguistic reorganization that Indian states were subjected to in the mid-fifties. Stress on language and ethnicity, he reckoned, would open a Pandora's box for a remote, sensitive region such as the Northeast. So he let the hill regions stay with. But now he bitterly complains of how Reangs have been intimidated, their women raped and men killed by the NLFT. Assam and the two former princely states Manipur and

Tripura were administered as Union Territories from Delhi. But the Naga insurrection forced Delhi to create the Nagaland state to take the steam out of the armed uprising. Once a million Nagas got a separate state, other ethnicities, some more populous than the Nagas, were to make similar demands. When refused, they would do what the Nagas did challenge the Indian state with arms.

In the last five or more decades after Partition, the Northeast has been India's most sustained insurgency theater. The intensity and the focus of the movements have changed over the years, and a number of the movements have been co-opted by the Indian state through power-sharing arrangements. But the call to arms has remained a popular option with the battling ethnicities of the Northeast either in challenging Delhi or while settling scores among themselves. And quite often, a number of armed movements in the region have used separatist rhetoric, despite being essentially autonomist or nativist in character, merely to attract attention in Delhi. Once India carved out the state of Nagaland in 1963, Assam's role as a sub-regional hegemon was threatened, its position as India's political subcontractor in the Northeast destined to end. Within a decade of the creation of the Nagaland state, Delhi had to affect a political reorganization of the whole region, through which three new administrative units were formed. These three became full-fledged states in the 1980s, as India desperately sought to control violent ethnic insurgencies in the area. On the other hand, the breakup of Assam not only produced fresh demands for ethnic homelands within what remained of it, but it also drove a section of the ethnic Assamese to insurgency. With the hills gone, the Assamese turned to their valleys to find they were fast becoming a minority there. The anti-foreigner movement rocked Assam between 1979 and 1985 and led to large-scale, free-for all types of ethnic riots. The ULFA, now the leading separatist organization in Assam, was born out of this movement. Its initial credo was ethnic cleansing it sought by the force of arms to drive the "foreigners" out of Assam. TNV fought for an "independent Tripura" but came to a settlement with Delhi in 1988 after it agreed to reserve a mere three additional legislative assembly seats for tribals. Such instances of using "secessionism" more as rhetoric than as a matter of conviction abound in the Northeast.

But over time, the ULFA's politics has changed. Sheltered in Bangladesh, Burma and Bhutan, and having to face the military might of the Indian state, the ULFA has denounced the Assam movement as "one that was led by juveniles, who failed to understand that migration per se was not bad and had helped many countries like the U.S.A. to become what they are today." The ULFA says that the Bengalis Hindus and Muslims alike have "immensely contributed to Assam" and "those of them who feel themselves as part of Assam should be treated as its legitimate dwellers." It is difficult to ascertain how much of this policy shift projecting itself as the "representative of the Asombashis" (dwellers of Assam) rather than the Asomiyas (Assamese) stems from tactical considerations such as seeking shelter in Bangladesh and gaining the support of Assam's huge Bengali population, and how much of it is a genuine attempt to rise above the ethnic considerations to forge a secular, multi-ethnic identity to fight Delhi. But the ULFA is being pragmatic only in trying to project territory and a multi-ethnic credo as the basis for a future independent Assam. It is only acknowledging the polyglot nature of the state of Assam and the rest of the region despite its broad racial difference with the Indian mainland. It is seeking to restore the multi-ethnic and assimilative nature of the Assamese nationality formation process, which was ruptured by racial-linguistic chauvinism of the upper-caste Assamese power-holder elites in the 1960s, as a result of which tribe after tribe exercised the exit option from Assam, fueling the demands of an ever-increasing number of ethnicity-based states in northeast India. Significantly, though the ULFA has targeted Hindi-speaking populations for large-scale attacks after 1990, it has avoided any attack on Bengalis, Nepalis or tribal groups that it sees as potential allies in the struggle against "Indian colonialism." The Hindi speakers have been seen as "Indian populations supportive of the colonial rule." But its growing lack of faith in ethnicity as the basis for its political militancy stems from a realization that there could be no "pure ethnic homeland" in Assam or anywhere else in northeast India.

Assamese nationalism, unless it caters to the distinct ethnic aspirations of the tribes and other communities in Assam, is a non-starter. The ULFA therefore, shrewdly enough, projects a future independent Assam as a federal Assam, where Bodo, Karbi, Dimasa, Rabha, Lalung or Mishing, or even Bengali homelands can exist, so long as the "basic values of Assamese society and culture are accepted." A security adviser to the Assam government describes this as "a clever ploy to broaden the support base of the ULFA insurgency against India." But Assam's political leadership now talks the same language, of the need to accept the polyglot character of Assam, and of satisfying the aspirations of the ethnic, linguistic and religious minorities, if not for anything else, only to stave off another breakup of the state. So, though ethnicity has been the mainstay of separatist movements and often formed the basis for the creation of political-administrative units in northeast India, its self-corrosive propensities have restricted the growth of local nationalisms strong enough to confront Delhi. Meghalaya came into being as a tribal state; today the three major tribes, Khasis, Jaintias and Garos, fight for the spoils of political office on ethnic lines, while some militant organizations such as the Achik National Volunteer Council are fighting for a separate state for the Garos. Mizoram has problems with its ethnic minorities. The Reangs and Chakmas tribes complain of ethnic and religious persecution and allege that the dominant Mizos, almost wholly Christian, want to convert them to Christianity and the Mizo way of life. The Lais and Maras want to join the Reangs and the Chakmas to form a separate unit, a Union Territory, which they want to be administered from the Centre. The Naga-Kuki clashes throughout northeast India that left hundreds of dead in the 1980s and 1990s raised the specter of Bosnia of how conflicting homeland demands could lead to ethnic cleansing in pursuit of the impossible creation of "pure ethnic states." Pradyut Bordoloi (then Assam's Minister of State for Home), 29 March, 2002 described Assam as a "multi-racial, multiethnic, multi-lingual and a multi-religious entity."

Memorandum jointly submitted by the Lai, Mara and Chakmas district councils to the Indian government on 17 August 2000. In some parts of what became India's Northeast, Communist parties subtly articulated ethnic issues to create a support base among the indigenous tribal people. In Tripura, the Communists played on the tribal's sense of loss and marginalization following the end of sovereign princely rule and the kingdom's merger with India. Having first secured popularity in the tribal areas through a powerful literacy movement (Jana Shiksha or Mass Literacy), the Communist Party of India (CPI) absorbed into its fold the main tribal organization, Gana Mukti Parishad, at the peak of its nationwide armed struggle in 1948. The CPI adopted the Parishad's political program as its own on questions of tribal rights, loss of tribal lands and the threat to the distinctive social organization of the tribes people but avoided demanding secession. Hundreds of Parishad activists and leaders turned into Communist guerrillas and fought "for the Indian revolution" rather than for an independent homeland like the Nagas. But when the CPI gave up armed struggle and purged those advocating the "adventurist line," the tribal guerrillas in the Communist force, Shanti Sena (Peace Army), gave up their weapons and returned to normal life. And taking advantage of the situation, the Congress dominated state administration started resettling the newly arrived Bengali migrants in large numbers in the tribal-compact areas of Tripura. Since the tribal people were largely supportive of the Communists, the Congress wanted to alter the demographic profile of the constituencies by promoting the organized rehabilitation of the Bengali migrants. It did help the Congress it won both the parliament seats in 1967 after losing them to the Communists in three successive elections but as the tribals lost out in the number's game, they lost faith in the Communist party and began to turn to militant ethnic politics. Having first manipulated ethnic concerns to build up a party nucleus and political base, the Communists succumbed to electoral concerns in Tripura. With other tribal parties and insurgent organizations surfacing to articulate the ethnic issues, the Communists have fallen back on their support base among the Bengalis. Since 1978, they have won all but one of the state assembly elections, but their popular base in the tribal areas has taken a beating. In 2000, for the first time, the ruling Communists lost the state's Tribal Areas Autonomous District Council to a militant tribal party, the Indigenous Peoples Front of Tripura (IPFT). The IPFT enjoyed the backing of the separatist National Liberation Front of Tripura (NLFT). The NLFT's rhetoric is secessionist but its leaders have said they are open to negotiations on an "appropriate power-sharing arrangement for maximum possible tribal control in the state assembly, the autonomous district council and on the state's resources."

On the eve of Independence of India, several ethnic groups had variously made effective use of the factors of ethnicity and regionalism as basis of ethnic rage, and democratic struggle for self-rule, greater autonomy and militant actions. Other factors such as frontier location, development process, rise of Christianity and democratic process, partition of country, influx of infiltrators and minority syndrome variously led to claims of separatism among the communities. In order to protect and preserve of the hill ethnic tribal population in the region special provisions were felt necessary which led the Constitution Drafting Committee of independent India to set up a sub-committee as "The North East Frontier Tribal and Excluded Areas Committee" in 1947. In 1948 the sub-committee recommended the creation of 'autonomous districts' and 'autonomous regions' to safeguard the hill tribes in respect of their land, social customs, language, and culture. These special recommendations were also incorporated into the Sixth Schedule of the Constitution. Accordingly, in 1952 autonomous district councils were constituted in the erstwhile Assam's districts of United Khasi-Jaintia Hills, Garo Hills, Lushai-Mizo Hills, Mikir Hills, and North Cachar Hills. At that time the plain tribal areas were notified as tribal belts and tribal blocks under the Assam Land and Revenue Regulation Act, 1886, ostensibly to protect the plain tribes from encroachments by the non-tribal population in their areas. The Naga movement, in which both ethnicity and extreme nationalism were used as operational strategies, is regarded as the mother of all movements in northeast India. The Naga insurgency started much before India's independence with the formation of the Naga National Council (NNC) under the legendary Angami Zapu Phizo. In 1951 the NNC established a sovereign Naga state which apparently came through a referendum that has never been accepted by the government. After several attempts by India at peace making, including the carving out of a separate Naga State in 1960 failed, the Indian Government responded with its military might which forced Phizo to escape via Bangladesh to London in 1960. This episode in the Nagas history also marked the beginning of the imposition of the controversial Armed Forces Special Powers Act (AFSA), 1958 in India's northeast.

The region has seen much violence since Independence. In response to demands by several tribes, ranging from separation from the Indian Union to various structures of self-governance, the state of Assam, which once constituted a major part of Northeast India, was reorganized to facilitate the creation of new states viz., Nagaland, Meghalaya, Mizoram, and Arunachal Pradesh. Even several territorially defined tribal councils were established in Assam and therefore, these experiments made encouragement to fulfill the aspirations of the various tribal groups, with several of them seeking to demarcate an exclusive territory and political space for themselves. Ethnic conflicts in northeast originally grew essentially through primordial affiliations. The distinctive ethnicity factor amongst communities led to steady expansion of aggressive binary categories of in-group and out-group (Das 2007). Insurgency in Assam is an offshoot of the anti-foreigners movement, primarily against the influx of migrants from Bangladesh that was started in 1979 by the All Assam Students Union (AASU). Violent communal agitations and riots broke out during the later part of 1979 which were particularly targeted against Muslim migrants of Bengali origin. During this six years of movement of All Assam Stüdent's Union both All Bodo Students Union and other Bodo allied organizations and political leaders extended full support to All Assam Students Union leaders in their anti-foreigners movement for the greater interest of the state of Assam (Chattopadhyay, 1990). Assam witnessed a worst ever violent movement in 1980s and 1990s by All Assam Students Union and Bodo movement. The agitation led to the loss of several hundreds of lives and of a considerable number of public and private properties. Estimation can be made that about two thousand people were killed, seventy thousand people were displaced and many common people suffered a lot due to the agitation (Bhagawati, 2002). Moreover, more than ten thousand Bengalis, Hindus and Muslims were displaced all over Assam in violence unleashed during the 1960s, 1970s and 1980s, particularly during six years of anti foreigner's agitation led by students union and the dominant Asamiyas. During the worst phase of violence in July-September 1960, almost 50,000 Bengalis, mostly Hindus crossed over to West Bengal seeking shelter there. Again, in 1972-73, 14000 Bengalis fled to West Bengal and elsewhere after the breakout of riots over language issue. However, the real figure of displacement as well as killed is far more than mentioned here because government account includes only those people who took refuge in the camps of West Bengal. Thousands died in the riots during the agitation between 1979 and 1985 where almost 2,000 in the village of Nellie alone (Bhaumik, 2005, Hussain, 2000). The movement causes to inter-ethnic clashes in the Bodo heartland of Kokrajhar and Bongaigaon has displaced a large number of people. It should also be mentioned here that the Bodo-Muslim ethnic violence that occurred in October 1993 has displaced about 3568 families consisting of 18000 persons. Again, a series of major incidents took place throughout the district in May 1996. This confli has resulted in the displacement of a huge population. Almost 42,214 families consisting of about 2, 62682 persons were displaced by this conflict. Ultimately their movement came to an end with the signing of the Assam Accord on 15th August1985 under the initiative of the then Prime Minister Rajiv Gandhi. In accordance with the terms of the said Accord, the congress Ministry of Assam resigned, the Assembly was dissolved and a fresh general election was held. The All Assam Students Union leaders who had already passed their students status formed a new regïonal political party Assam Gana Parighat and participated in the election under the banner of the new party. As expected they won with a very comfortable majority and formed the new Assam Government. The Bodos were also participants in the All Assam Students Union movement and expected the Assam Gana Parishad government to realize their grievance. As the post accord euphoria died down, the Bodos and other tribal felt that the attention of

Assam Gana Parishad Government to tribal was no different from the earlier ones. As disillusionment spread among the Bodos and non-Bodos relations in tribal area deteriorated.

The objectives of All Assam Students Union movement were to drive out foreigners from Assam and to bring peace to the state by preserving the identities of various ethnic groups and tribal people in the state. After coming to power the Assam Gana Parishad Government tried their best to promote only the Assamese language and culture in total exclusion of any other indigenous group and their language and culture in total violation of the Clause 6 of Assam Accord. The ABSU leaders and leaders of other Bodo allied organizations naturally took it as complete negation of the composite and diverse cultural and linguistic milieu of Assam (Roy, 1995). The other clause of the Accord provided for strict enforcement of all relevant laws to ensure prevention of encroachment on lands of tribal people and that of Government lands. The string of violent conflicts that rocked Assam for almost two decades were movements led by a number of tribal groups called Bodos in Western Assam. The main issues were dispossession from their lands by Bengali and Assamese settlers, as well as neglect of the Bodo language and culture. The Bodo movement which was quelled following successful peace negotiations between different factions of the Bodo insurgencies was marked by extensive violence that saw buses, trains and railway lines being blown up at regular intervals. Since the 1990s a number of militant organizations have continued to mushroom in Assam where most of it on the lines of identity, religion and culture. Currently, there are as many as 34 insurgent groups listed in the State, though the ULFA is the main player. Among other terrorist outfits, the National Democratic Front of Bodoland (NDFB), Bodo Liberation Tigers (BLT), United People's Democratic Solidarity (UPDS), Dima Halam Daoga (DHD), and Muslim United Liberation Tigers of Assam (MULTA) are prominent.

Every State in the region is currently affected by insurgent and terrorist violence and the states like Assam, Manipur, Nagaland and Tripura witness scales of conflict that can be categorized as low intensity wars, defined as conflicts in which fatalities are over 100 but less than 1000 per annum. Insurgency and counter-insurgency has claimed over 40,000 lives since 1979 though the numbers could be much more than what is officially reflected. Over 1,000 people were reported killed throughout this region in 2007 including 453 civilians, 65 security personnel, and 501 militants. Assam, Manipur and Nagaland continued to be the areas with the largest number of casualties with Assam recording 437 deaths, Manipur 408, and Nagaland, 108.

Before the *British Rule*, Bodo-*Kachari Kingdom* may have included a vast area extending far and beyond *Assam,* a small province in the *North-East India.* History suggests that *Dimapur* was the capital of Bodo-Kachari kingdom (*Dimasa* Kachari kingdom). The British-India colonial rulers effectively adopted different policies which were not suited to the ethnic population in the country which caused them to remain far distance from the main stream. This has been likely that Bodo-Kachari were lagging behind their fellow Indians in terms of many aspects particularly in education. Since the time of *British Rule, Assam* was known to produce oil, natural gas, *tea* plantation. However, in comparison to other parts of India and even nearby state such as *West Bengal* opportunity for general and mass education came to North East India only after Indian independence. After independence Bodos were given the opportunity to take advantage of *scheduled tribe* (ST) status and this process lead to the creation of tribal belts and blocks, protected lands meant for farming and grazing, specifically for the *Bodo people*.

In the 1960s the *Plains Tribal Council of Assam* (PTCA), a political party representing Bodos and other plains tribal of Assam realized that tribal belts and blocks were gradually being acquired by rich landlords or new immigrants through illegal means. Moreover, Bodos had little or no access to economic aid that was given by the central government. Without economic package to the Bodo dominated areas, education was a distant cry. In those days, there were hardly any roads and other infrastructures that connected Bodo dominated area to the main cities of *Assam*. These were the reasons for which PTCA demanded a Union Territory called *Udayachal,* to be carved out of Assam. The proposed Udayachal map included mainly those areas that were known as tribal belts and blocks. The creation of tribal belts and blocks meant for scheduled-tribes was a mechanism to protect farming and grazing lands mainly from rich landlord and illegal immigrants. However, the demand for Udayachal never materialized. Many parties came to power, thus players changed and so did the game. By the end of 70's it became clear that Bodos had a little or no influence in the Indian political process. The demand for creation of a homeland for the plains tribal of Bodos in the shape of Udayachal became a major blank of political movement by the Bodos during the seventies and their peaceful movement turned out to be a violent one and thus invited police action. The party could not do anything even after lapse of seventeen years since its formation. The common people lost their confidence in the organization and started to reject the same. The emergence of All Bodo Students Union is the beginning of the emergence of political consciousness among the Bodos as well as the tribal of Assam. The first tribal political party also came into being in 1967 only under the initiative of the All Bodo Students Union. It has big role in the awakening of linguistic and socio-cultural movement of plains tribal people of Assam and some parts of the country. Ironically, though All Bodo Students Union was known as non political student's body it was compelled to lead some movement which has been a political nature. During the period of 1972 to 1980 the All Bodo Students Union led the land restoration movement to get back the lands from illegal immigrants who illegally occupied tribal land in the tribal belts and blocks area. It was under the British rule that the Bodos first raised separate electoral roll of Bodos which can be treated as the symptom of the demand for a separate homeland along with hill tribes of the north-east India.

Even after independence, for several decades, higher education was out of reach for most Bodos. Universities and higher educational institutes are located in faraway places such as *Guwahati,* and *Dibrugarh*. Moreover, year after year majority Bodo students were not admitted to some of the best educational institutes in Assam like *Cotton College, Assam Agricultural University, Assam Engineering College* and *Gauhati University*. In addition, even after obtaining university diplomas, Bodo youngsters had limited or no job opportunities. These reasons fueled disappointments among many Bodo students. Although, Bodos were given ST quota, most of those jobs or opportunities often went unfilled. Every office in Assam was filled with *Assamese* speaking people, from high ranking officers down to simple office peons. Creating easier educational opportunities for Bodos became first goal for ABSU. When the *All Assam Students Union's* (AASU) agitation to drive out illegal immigrants (during 1979-85) was slowing down, the demand for a separate state called the Bodoland was gaining momentum. The demand solely depends on the so-called equal rights for everyone as described in constitution of *India*.

Specifically, in *Assam* Bodos areas were very much neglected. Often the financial packages meant for tribal-development were diverted and misused. For similar reasons, Khasis and Garos carved out *Meghalaya* from Assam. During 1980s, All Bodo Students' Union's (*ABSU*) became very concerned about decades of neglect and apathy by the subsequent state government towards the Bodo community. ABSU and Bodo political parties jointly demanded a separate state, called *Bodoland.* The official Bodoland Movement for an independent state of Bodoland started on March 2, 1987 under the leadership of *Upendranath Brahma* of the *All Bodo Students' Union* (ABSU). The ABSU created a political organization, the Bodo Peoples' Action Committee (BPAC), to spearhead the movement. The ABSU/BPAC movement began with the slogan "Divide Assam fifty-fifty". The ABSU/BPAC leadership of the movement ended with the bipartite Bodo Accord of February 20, 1993 and the creation of the BAC. The accord soon collapsed amidst a vertical split in ABSU and other Bodo political parties.

Despite the Bodo accord, neglect remains, with no economic improvement is evident in Bodo dominated areas. Lately, there have been few signs of efforts to improve these situations. However, there are thousands of people still languishing in refugee camps in very poor conditions. Their lives have been disrupted several times in last two decades. Among the Bodos consciousness gradually took a definite form and developed to the stage of demanding statehood for Bodoland in order to safeguard the interest of Bodos through political means. Ultimately after a long 10 years of movement the time came for signing of Bodo Accord-II on 10th February 2003 with which Bodoland Territorial Council (BTC) or Bodoland Territorial Area District (BTAD) comprising all the 3082 villages was created with an amendment under the Sixth Schedule of the Constitution of India. The Bodoland Territorial Area District constituted in 2003 is the latest autonomous council to have been constituted under the provisions of the Sixth Schedule. The Bodoland Territorial Area District has an area of 8970 sq.km which is about 11.4 per cent of the total geographical area of Assam. There are four newly created districts under the Council, namely Kokrajhar, Chirang, Baksa and Udalguri. These districts have been carved out from the original district of Kokrajhar, Dhubri, Bongaigaon, Barpeta, Nalbari, Kamrup, Darrang and Sonitpur. There are ten Sub-Divisions including district head quarters, 33 Development Blocks, 415 Village Council Development Committee and 3082 Villages under the Council.

The formation of the Bodoland Territorial Area District is a consequent of a long drawn movement for creation of a separate state for the Bodos, one of the largest plain tribes of Assam. Initially in 1993, an agreement was reached between centre and state government and representatives of the Bodo community, which led to the formation of the Bodoland Autonomous Council constituted under the Bodoland Autonomous Council Act of 1993 (Assam Act of 1993). However, right from the start, the functioning of the Bodoland Autonomous Council was marred by serious ambiguity regarding the territorial jurisdiction and also the powers and function of the council. This led to re-emergence of the demand for separate statehood. Finally, on 10th of February 2003, after series of rounds of negotiation, a memorandum of understanding was signed amongst the central government, state government and the Bodo Liberation Tiger for creation of Bodoland Territorial Council under the Sixth Schedule of the Constitution. Consequent to this agreement, the sixth schedule to the constitution (Amendment) Act, 2003, was passed by parliament and the Bodoland Territorial Council was constituted as per the provisions of the Sixth Schedule. Accordingly, the Bodoland Territorial Area District (BTAD) was added to as item No. 3 of Part1 of the table appended to Paragraph 20 of the Sixth Schedule of the Constitution.

The Bodo movement initially included 92 demands of many points of vital interests to the Bodos and for the time being all demands were given less importance in favour of three principal political demands. These are as follows:

- Creation of a separate state called "Bodoland" on the north bank of the river Brahmaputra.

- Creation of autonomous district councils in the tribal dominated areas on the south bank of the Brahmaputra.
- Inclusion of 'Bodo-Kacharis' of Karbi Anglong in the Sixth Schedule of the Constitution of India.

Bodo Movement through the Lens of Human Development

Human Development is defined as expansion of human capabilities. This new paradigm of development advocates an alternative model that is drawn on cultural heritage of a society and borrow from others when possible and useful (Nurse, 2007). The international experience of the last few decades seems to suggest that there is some kind of association between the level of identity concerns and expansion of human development. The societies with comparatively higher penetration by other cultures have remained most vulnerable and dependent in spite of some brief periods of rapid growth. However, their economic prosperity has proved to be unsustainable and highly unequal leading to inter-ethnic and class conflict, totalitarianism and military strive in worst cases. Although the concept of human development (HD) measures of socio-economic progress of a nation/ state/ district/ block and it has been measured in the form of a composite index called as Human Development Index (HDI) incorporate only three dimensions as life expectancy, real Gross Domestic Product (GDP) per capita and educational attainment reflecting the human achievement. The composite index Human Development Index intends to capture three most critical dimensions of human well-being: health, education and income. The first Human Development Report launched by United Nations Development Program (UNDP) in 1990, defined human development as a process of enlarging people's choices. These choices cover social, political, psychological and other aspects of human life. However, for the sake of simplicity only three essential choices viz., to lead a healthy and long life, to acquire knowledge and to have access to the resources needed for a decent standard of living are incorporated in Human Development Index. The other important choices of human life such as human rights, political participation etc is not incorporated because of the complexity in doing so. For this the Human Development Index is often described as the poor representing the vast concept of human development. However, there are studies across the globe which attempt to add the other area of these aspects of human life into the measurement of human development.

People's choices may vary according to ethnic group, religion, place of residence etc. Even the people belonging to the same ethnic group or religion may differ in choices according to place of residence, level of education, economic status etc. Human rights such as fundamental rights of human being as access to food, cloth, shelter, housing, freedom of speech, freedom of movement, freedom of shelter, political participation, education, employment, preservation of own language, religion, custom and culture etc are essential choices/freedom to measure the welfare of the human being. When these basic human rights are denied to the people/ citizens of a democratic country, when superior class of community relatively seem to enjoy greater of such basic rights over the other, there being uprising against the other.

This is what happens to the Bodos in Assam. The Bodo as the origin inhabitants of the Brahmaputra Valley ruled the entire valley with glorious past, however, they lost their land to the Ahoms in the 13th Century, now tried to regain their lost land with a view to preserve their identity, language, religion and culture. Long time denied to them regarding their language, religion, custom and tradition led them to rethink differently in the beginning of the twentieth century. Preservation of language, identity, religion and culture were the prime concerns to the Bodos in the early part of the twentieth century. They therefore, started their ethnic based movement at the early part of the twenty century with the submission of memorandum to the Simon Commission demanding separate electorate roll for the Bodos. In 1933 the Tribal League, a sociopolitical organization, was formed to highlight the socioeconomic problems of the plain tribals of Assam. This development has been largely attributed to the swift pace of modernization and democratization. Initially Bodo movement was started as a socio-cultural movement amongst the Bodos-Kacharis tribe, had the avowed goal of securing their cultural, socio-economic rights. Subsequently, the movement now has developed into a socio-political movement, demanding a separate state for the Bodos within the Indian union.

However, with the formation of Bodo Sahitya Sabha in 1952, clash of interest started between mainstream Assamese nationalism and Bodo nationality, both in ideological, socio-cultural, linguistic and lastly in political level. So long Bodo Sahitya Sabha was not in existence, the trends of the construction and development of Assamese nationality moved up unaffected and flourished into high level. The Bodo Sahitya Sabha was founded initially keeping three important objectives in view like creation of common Bodo language and literature by synthesing Dimacha and Bodo languages, upgradation of Bodo as the medium of instruction and development of Bodo culture and construction of Bodo nationality through literary works. Under the initiative of Bodo Sahitya Sabha, Bodos in Assam got platform to develop Bodo language and literature which had encouraged them to take education in their mother tongue. Bodo students and youth of middle classes who had received education through their mother tongue woke up and realized that identity assertion has been very important to survive in the world. Literate persons among Bodos were very negligible since independence. However, literate persons were on increasing trend among them since the formation of Bodo Sahitya Sabha. As per 1991 Census, among Bodos, literacy rate was 41.15 per cent which was increased to 51.48 per cent in 2001. Since Assam is one of the most ethnically diverse states in the country a number of ethnic groups are living in the state. Where total tribal population in the state, according to the Census of India 2001, has been recorded as 33,08,570 accounting for 12.41 per cent of state population. Among the main tribes of Assam, Bodos and Miris together account for roughly half of the total tribal population of the state. Bodos alone constitute about 41 per cent of the total tribal population, followed by Miris with 18 per cent, Karbis with 11 per cent and Sonowal Kachari with 7 per cent.

It is the Bodo Sahitya Sabha which has been playing a pivotal role in the development of Bodo language and literature. The objectives of Bodo Sahitya Sabha were to develop and expand Bodo language by introducing it as the medium of instruction for the Bodo children. With this view the Bodo Sahitya Sabha launched several movements since its inception. The demand was finally conceded during the Chief Ministership of Bimala Prasad Chaliha in 1962. Accordingly Bodo language was first introduced as medium of instruction in 1963 in L.P. schools of Kokrajhar sub-division only. Since then the Bodo language has not looked back. On the demands of Bodo people in general and Bodo Sahitya Sabha in particular Bodo language was introduced as the medium of instruction up to secondary stage in different schools of Assam. In 1973 Bodo language was introduced as Major Indian Language in Gauhati, Dibrugarh and North Eastern Hill University. It was the youth and educated middle class of Bodo people among whom ethnic identity assertion, preservation of language, religion and culture were injected into their mind during eighties. The All Bodo Students Union was founded in 1967 and the birth of Plains Tribal Council of Assam, a Bodo political organization in the same year, with the support of Bodo Sahitya Sabha and other Bodo allied organizations initially demanded the creation of an autonomous region exclusively for the plain tribes Bodos of Assam; a demand it then revised in favour of a Union Territory. However, the search for distinct linguistic identity for the Bodo people and their safeguard realized the creation of Bodoland Territorial Districts Area under the Sixth Schedule of the Indian Constitution in 2003 and Bodo language has been included in the eight schedule of the constitution of India. The movement was in the form of literary bent and socio-economic in nature but subsequently Bodo movement transformed into political one through which Bodo people tried to preserve their past glory. The present study reviews the movement through the lens of human development concept. It set the hypothesis that significant deprivation of Bodos over the years place the community at very low level of human development.

Research Questions

Research on development has become increasingly engaged with questions of political economy, ethno-cultural identity and also physical geography. A serious agenda in this regard has been to explore how political choices, institutional structure and form of governance influence the economic choices made by governments and citizens, and also how these choices shape patterns of economic development (Adam and Dercon, 2009). The primary concerns of the present study are to examine how abysmal progress in capability expansion can construct a culturo-political identity of its own over a period time and how to address such ethnic isolations for the broader interests of the nations.

The research problem needs concrete and specific defined area in which the research problem is to be studied. The area which has been undertaken for the purpose has to be relevant with the present context. The importance of the problems lies with the ground reality and would have to be relevant to be presented before the social scientists so that the defined problem could draw the attention in the society. Here, the study has presented political-economy of Bodo Movement in Assam and their human development status as research problem. An attempt has been made to examine how Bodo movement has justification for attaining autonomy or statehood and have examined socio-economic status of the Bodos and their human development indices so as to present the problem before the present complexity of society. The study, therefore, seeks to answer the following research questions:

- What is the status of Bodos in the expansion of human development?
- How far the existing level of human development is responsible for the mounting dissatisfactions in the minds of Bodos?
- What should be an appropriate policy decision for the amicable solution of the Bodo issues in Assam?

Organization of the Study

The study has been organised into seven chapters. After this Introductory Chapter which summarizes identity issues in modern development discourse, presents the historical background of Bodo Movement in Assam and seeks to view the movement through the lenses of human development. The remaining thesis is organized as follows:

Chapter two reviews the existing literature on Bodo community and their movement to capture a holistic profile of the political economy of the region. It covers a wide-ranging issues related to their socioeconomic conditions, linguistic and cultural heritage, ethnic aspects, political developments and a brief history of Bodo aspirations in pre- and post independence era. Chapter three draws the framework designed to carry out the present research study. It narrates the objectives of the study, sets the hypotheses, and discusses the methodology adopted to fulfill the objectives. This chapter also introduces the nature and sources of data used in this study to test the hypothesis.

Taking the stock of secondary information Chapter four intends to evaluate the status of human development of Bodo inhabited districts of Assam as compared to other districts. The purpose of this chapter is to present a comparative analysis of development indicators. First, identity of Bodos has been briefly introduced and secondly looked at the demographic profile of the state in such a fashion that the Bodo dominated settlements could be spotted. This section also discusses settlement of the Bodos along with the population characteristics as well as the demographic transition that had taken place in the state during 1990s. Next, captures the socioeconomic profile of these districts as compared to the state as a whole and finally summarized the status of human development in the state with special reference to Bodo-inhabited districts.

Chapter five deals with primary data to enumerate the status of human development of Bodo population living in the rural areas of Bodoland Territorial Area District(BTAD).Adopting the similar methodology of Human Development Report Assam (2003), this chapter constructs the Human Development Index for each of the sample villages. Adjusting them for sample errors Human Development Indices for all the four districts under BTAD as well as for the Bodos living in the areas under BTAD are obtained by applying standard statistical tools. Chapter six intends to capture the dynamics of Bodo aspiration on development and long-lasting movement through *Focus Group Discussions* (FGD). This chapter is based on the qualitative judgments of the respondents on the priorities and their understanding of well-beings, and thereby, capabilities.

Chapter seven decides about the hypotheses, set in Chapter three on the basis of the findings in Chapter four, five & six, and derives some policy recommendations. Finally presents the references at the end of the thesis and the questionnaire used for the collection of primary information.

2

Political Economy of Bodo Movement

The political economy of Bodo movement involves many issues which include socioeconomic as well as political ones. Bodos in Assam are trying hard to preserve their ethnic identity, language, socio-political rights, religion and culture through creation of a state namely *Bodoland.* An overall profile of the Bodo community has been presented in this Chapter for understanding the identity issues, apparently worked behind the Bodo movement.

Profile of Bodos

Socioeconomic Aspects

Over the years there have been some changes in the population distribution of Bodos in Assam. As far as the population is concerned there is about 43.19 per cent of tribal population of the state of which Bodo people were majority in 1951. The figure has been fluctuating from one Census year to another. In 1971, it was reduced to 40.11 per cent and then increased to 41.12 per cent in 1991. Again, in 2001 it marginally decreased to 40.89 per cent. In 2001, the percentage share of Bodo population among the total population of the state stands only 5.07 per cent whereas it was 5.28 per cent in 1991.The landscape of the study area Bodoland Territorial Area Districts is just about 11.34 per cent of the total area of the state whereas its population is nearly 11.24 per cent of the total state's population as per 2001 census. However, there is fluctuation over the years and this has been of course due to many reasons viz. in and out migration, massive infiltration of people from Bangladesh, re-organization of the state, census manipulation etc. All these have resulted in the change in demography pattern of Bodos in Bodo-dominated areas of the state. This has caused an alarm to the leaders of the movement.

Land to a tribal was a part of socioeconomic and cultural heritage. More than ninety five per cent of them are dependent upon agriculture and allied activities in the state. Land is the only tangible asset of a tribal family. The emotional ties with the land lie with the fact that it provides the burial ground for their ancestor th whom they would be united after death and sacrificial grove where they propitiated their spirits. There are a number of social and religious rituals connected with land, which establish emotional ties between the tribal and the lands. The ownership of land among them broadly falls under three categories, viz. (a) community land (b) land possessed by an individual, and (c) land belonging to a particular clan. In the absence of settlement or up-to-date record of land rights, they are at the mercy of petty officials of revenue and forest departments and the mighty landlords. When ninety five per cent of tribal people depend on agriculture about seventy per cent of them have become practically landless. One of the great suffering endured by them for generation has been the alienation of their ancestral land. The process of land alienation was aided initially by the government during colonial times. They were not granted permanent land rights partly because of the fact that many of them who were peasants were also migratory cultivators.

During fifties the state government of Assam under the Congress Govt. created a number of tribal belt and blocks in which only tribal and scheduled castes could own land, but the encroachments and land grabbing persisted. Various settlements policies of the successive state governments brought new settlers on the tribal land. The land transference to the non tribal or outsiders in the tribal belt and block began after the British came. But infect transference of tribal land in the hands of outsiders or non-tribal, especially money lenders and absentee landlords, started much before the advent of the British in the region. The Assam Land and Revenue Regulation Act, 1886 has the provision to control such illegal transfer of land but it was partially successful in its implementation. The so called protective measure of land provided in the Act was not enforced. The Bodo leaders alleged that besides this encroachment, the state Govt. had taken away about six lakhs acres for Govt. projects. The present Capital of the state, Dispur stands on land which once belonged to the tribal people. Mr. Thaneswar Boro, then Revenue Minister of Assam himself once admitted that two lakhs and thirteen thousand bighas of land in tribal belt and blocks were under illegal occupation of the non-tribal encroachers. As per the clause ten of the Assam Accord encroachment of lands is strictly to be prevented; unauthorized encroachers to be evicted and the relevant law to be enforced. When the Assam Gana Parishad leaders assumed office, the non-tribes were flourishing in their businesses in some pockets and they were in fact provided with the necessary infrastructure. Thus, unabated encroachment of land, increase in the number of landless tribal, unemployment and gradual deterioration of general economic conditions in spite of government developmental activities created discontentment among the tribal youths. Observing the situation, All Assam Students Union and All Bodo Students Union jointly demanded eviction of all non-tribes from the tribal belt and blocks.

Like land, forest is also intimately connected with tribal life. "It is the abode of the spirits, the place of worship" (Chattopadhay, 1988) and the seat of life cycle ceremonies including burial (sardhana). Forest provides the tribal with food, fuel, fertilizer, fodder, farm implements and material equipments for family use. Rope making by bamboo, thatch, rearing of animals, such as goat, cow, and gathering of fuel etc amply illustrate the importance of forest in tribal life. However, urbanization and industrialization along with tremendous growth of population both natural and migration reduction of landholding, pressures of money economy and the ingenuity of more advanced groups, made the situation desperate for the Bodo peasants who were compelled to move to the reserve forests and the traditional areas for their settlement and shifting cultivation. Even after moving to forests they were also not free from problems. Assam Gana Parishad government passed a law legitimizing eviction of unauthorized tribal who had settled in the forests and reserved areas. That is why Bodo people have been trying to preserve their own land rights and forest. The economy of the tribes is greatly dependent on collection and sale of wood and other minor forest produce. It is learnt that ten to twenty per cent of the income of an average tribe family in the major tribal concentration is obtained through the sale of the minor forest produce.

Occupational livelihood and employment refers to the aggregate distribution of *occupations* in society, classified according to skill level, economic function, or social status. The occupational structure is shaped by various factors such as the structure of the economy with the relative weight of different industries, *technology* and *bureaucracy* lying the distribution of technological skills and administrative responsibility, the *labour-market* which determines the pay and conditions attached to occupations, and by *status* and prestige as influenced by occupational *closure,* life-style, and social values. The occupational structure is described and analysed by means of various classificatory schemes, which group similar occupations together according to specific criteria such as skill, employment status, or function. Such classifications are also used as a basis for the empirical analysis of economic and social class. Getting occupational livelihood as well as employment becomes major problem among the plains tribes of Assam especially among Bodos because of low literacy as well as ignorance of parents towards education. Few Bodo youths who received higher education with great difficulties could not get good jobs by competing with other non-tribe educated youths who are economically and politically more powerful. In the state only ten per cent of jobs are reserved for the plains tribes, and appointments are made on the basis of party affiliation and other communal considerations. Even the state Govt. has set knowledge of Assamese language as a pre-requisite in state services without having any regards for Boro language, violating Article 15 and 16 of the Constitution and Clause No.7 of Assam Official Language Act, 1960. The Govt. has no answer for the backlog in the recruitment of tribal candidates to the third and fourth grade posts in state govt. Therefore, Bodos in Assam getting displeasure with the authority and has been agitating for separate homeland so as to avail various socio-economic opportunities in this circumstances.

Linguistic and Cultural Heritage

The language tangle is one of the most critical and sensitive issues confronting the Bodos in Assam. Assam is already polarized on ethnic and linguistic lines. Language is the most effective medium of exchanging views, ideas, culture and way of expression of human personality. As such, it is used by the people as a symbol of identity of their communities. Chatterjee (1974) lauded the Bodos for its richness in language and historicity. Hodgson used the word 'Bodo' for the first time to denote Bodo language and its speakers. Since then missionary researchers and writers have started taking keen interest and investigations into the origin and development of Bodo language. Missionary works on Bodo language and grammar had begun in 1797 and ended in 1959, the year of publication of Bodo grammar by Rev. H Holversrud.

However, Bodos do not have its own script and Bodo language has been written in Assamese script and alphabet. Bodo language has many dialects and so there noticed no uniform dialects to express common meaning to them in the vast area in the state. There was language and script movement during 1973-1974 where many Bodos have been sacrificed in the cause of language. However, the language and script movement came to an end with the adoption of Devanagri script. Since then Bodo language has got its new life which permits in writing Bodo modern writers their own language at Devanagri script. Creation of Bodo Sahitya Sabha (1952) has started clash of interest between Assamese nationality and Bodo nationality in ideologically, socio-cultural, linguistic and lastly in political line. As soon as Bodo Sahitya Sabha was in existence the trends of the construction and development of Assamese nationality got obstructed. Soon after its creation primary units of Bodo Sahitya Sabha came into existence in various places during 1952-1960 where its achievement was nothing specific but confined only to organizational development. The demand for Assamese as official language of entire Assam during 1960s exerted negative reactions on the non-Assamese people particularly amongst the hills people. The non-Assamese people or ethnic tribal people of Assam considered it as the policy of assamanisation through the imposition of Assamese language on non Assamese people. As a reaction to this move taken by Assamese speaking people the hill people demanded for retention of English as the official language in hill areas and the people of Barak valley demanded Bengali as the official language in Barak valley. The leaders of Bodo Sahitya Sabha opined that the implementation of language policy would divide Assam on language basis and hence demanded the govt. for implementation of Hindi language as the official language of Assam as an alternative language. Ultimately, the three language formula as Assamese in Assam, Bengali in Barak valley and English in hills area was accepted as viable alternative.

Bodo Sahitya Sabha since its inception worked strongly to unite Bodos on language basis and worked towards development of Bodo language. Demand was made to introduce Bodo language in the schools of Bodo dominated areas. Accordingly, Bodo as a medium of instruction was conceded after a prolonged agitation at the primary level in 1963 and subsequently in the secondary level of education and textbooks and other ancillary literary works were brought out in Bodo language. On the demands of Bodo people in general and Bodo Sahitya Sabha in particular Bodo language was introduced as the medium of instruction up to secondary stage in different schools of Assam. In 1973 Bodo language was introduced as Major Indian Language in Gauhati, Dibrugarh and North Eastern Hill University.

Bodo has its own rich culture and language. They had past glorious and ruled over the entire Brahmaputra valley. Over the time they lost everything from their possession. However, Bodo were on the virgin of extinction before the emergence of British rule in India. The impact of modern civilization installed by the British government in India like introduction of modern education based on science and technology and introduction of new economic system against the static traditional caste based economy and the emergence of employment avenues to the people and social mobility irrespective of caste and religions, advancement of transport and communication, effective new administrative and political system, introduction of rules of law and new legal system treating all section of people equal before the law and protection of the rights of the disadvantages society were the forces awakening the Bodo society. The effect of the introduction of modern culture and civilization was far reaching. This has installed the sense of self respect and socio-cultural, political, economic consciousness amongst all sections of people in their own ways. This has also created identity consciousness based on ethnicity, race, language and religion.

Bodo language being the mother language of Bodo community and as medium of instruction in the state of Assam, the govt. ignoring other ethnic group of population, Assamese language was trusted upon the non Assamese population including the indigenous tribes. As a result of this many non tribal population in the state make hue and cry and because of this reason Bodo movement initially had a literary bent turned into political one. Though Bodo language was conceded, the Assamese script was thrust upon the Bodos. This was objected through various agitations in the early seventies and demand was made for Roman script. A settlement was made for the Devnagari script in 1976. Further, just after assuming power the Assam Gana Parighat government imposed Assamese language as compulsory third language in all the secondary schools through a circular given by the Secondary Board of Education of Assam on 28th February 1986. This incensed the Bodos and other non-Assamese communities in the state. Though it was later revoked, the Bodos felt of being dominated by the majority in the pretext of Assamese as a regional language and the official language of the state linking different communities within it. The Aghom Gana Parighat government also issued notification making the knowledge of Assamese, a pre condition for employment in Assam State Services violating the Assam Official Language (Amendment) Act, 1985 by which Bodo was recognized as associate official language in Bodo dominated areas. So, the policies of the Government hampered the employment avenues of Bodo students educated in medium of instruction other than Assamese.

Ethnic and Cultural Solidarity

Bodos have a genuine aspiration to establish a distinct Bodo nationality and to get recognition in the world as a civilized society and an advanced nationality. Basic question that arises is that of their survival, and preservation and growth of their ethnic identity. They feel that they have no chance of preserving their own culture and heritage in the present setup and atmosphere and therefore they resented towards state administration. They neither wanted to share their territory with other ethnic groups nor recognized the government of the state to represent their interest and aspirations. The perception among them of having their own heritage and culture is deep rooted; and their urge to preserve the Bodo identity has come in sharp conflict with the attempt of the Assamese people to maintain their language, culture and political domination. Since various ethnic groups in the north eastern region and other parts of the country have been allowed to maintain their distinctive identity through ages the demand for such type of identity by Bodos is quite obvious and justified. In fact smaller states were carved out from Assam on the basis of ethnic considerations. For examples, Mizos got Mizoram, Khasis, Jaintias and Garos got Meghalaya, Nagas got Nagaland, Manipuris got Manipur in the northeastern region. Similarly, outside the northeastern region, Bengalis got West Bengal, Oriyas got Orissa, Telugus got Andhra Pradesh, Tamilians got Tamil Nadu, Marathis got Maharashtra, Gujaratis got Gujarat, and Punjabis got Punjab etc.

The Bodo culture attained its distinctiveness over the years marked by a close relationship between nature and man, egalitarianism social structure, accommodative history, equal sharing of economy, secularism, religious pursuits, a demographic political thinking and a people oriented art and literature. Since they are not isolated from the surrounding of non tribal societies and modernization are now vulnerable to outside influence. Such contacts with outside world have created dilemma in their life and culture resulting into an identity crisis. Neither are they able to acclimatize to the urban and alien values, nor are they in a position to preserve and pursue their own traditional rites, rituals and customs. They are also gradually losing their identity because of their accommodative nature and readiness to mix with outsiders.

Bodos are the worshippers of nature, but a large scale devastation of forests in the name of rapid industrialization, urbanization and consequent upon social forestry schemes, plantation of indigenous varieties mostly non-indigenous in nature, quick growing trees have adversely affected their life pattern and religious beliefs. Traditional tribal religions such as animism, saran-dharam of nature worshiping are gradually being replaced by Christianity, Hinduism and others. Changes in the food habits of Bodos and their festivals are also quite evident. Bodos, for instance, are abstaining from beef eating and seem to be less interested in celebrating as a result of their close proximity with enamoring Hindu society. Possessing a very rich tradition of their own, they are thus, not only denying themselves of a rich protein diet but also sacrificing their age old cultural heritage. Besides, the Bodo society, traditionally known for its egalitarianism, is being divided today on religion lines and even on communal lines. Agriculture has been increasingly receiving a mere sub-servant type of status of other occupations like business and industry, services.

As a matter of fact, the tribal, especially the Bodo community unable to cope with the external pressure from all sides, are a frustrated lot and as a natural consequence developing marks of a negative identity of themselves. They feel that they are being branded by the civilized world as lazy indiscipline people, underdeveloped and uncivilized. Thus, the notions of a noble, savage and a healthy tribe were fast becoming myth. These signs of cultural degradation sometimes generate among the tribal a common psychology of identity assertion for their own survival.

Political Developments

Bodos are not socially and politically conscious. They were not at all conscious regarding even their past glorious culture and language. However, during the British rule the Bodo first raised a separate electorate roll of their community and this was the first time to get separate identity before the British Govt. along with hill tribes of the north-east India. Political consciousness came to the Bodos with the formation of Plains Tribal Council of Assam in 1967 and a powerful student's organisation which is known as All Bodo Students Union also got birth in the same year. This was the turning point towards the Bodos for getting self consciousness and self determination. Slowly and gradually the Bodos have realized their socio-economic problems and they thought intro-spectively. Understanding their present political scenario, the Bodos in Assam at present being a political minority; they take direct part in the politics of the country through a few reserved constituencies. The faulty delimitation and the democratic change brought about by the coming of new settlers have reduced them to an ineffective minority in many of these constituencies. The system of parliamentary democracy and government is based on the principle of majority votes polled and seats secured. In matters of polling majority votes, Bodos in Assam can never expect to win in any assembly or parliamentary constituency, even by casting hundred per cent votes, because even in reserved constituencies, tribal voters are slightly higher than thirty per cent only. This is because constituencies have been craftily delimitated by cutting away compact tribal inhabited areas into several portions and tagging them into non-schedule tribe majority constituencies in order to deprive them from sending their genuine representative to the assembly and parliament.

The political development of the seventies in India made the tribal people in their introspection to think differently. The State Reorganization Act 1971 and Art. 244 (A) of the Constitution empowers the Central Government to grant limited authority to the hill districts of Assam for the protection of the hill tribes and retention of their socio-economic and political identities. Ironically, plains tribes were totally excluded from the purview of Art. 244 (A) and thus were being constitutionally discriminated though the tribal of Karbi-Anglong and North Cachar Hills were provided with limited autonomy through formation of autonomous district councils. What has happened today has been due to the policy of the Government of India towards tribes. In the sixties some of the hill districts of Assam with four to five lakhs of population were granted with statehood, the Bodos with around 13 lakhs of population were denied such entitlement. As we know the Govt. of India agreed to provide the Assamese society adequate constitutional, legal and administrative safeguard in the Assam Accord. The Accord, however, does not mention about the need for safeguards to minority communities and weaker sections like Bodos. They feel that the majority community in the state never accepted them as part of the Assamese community and society in true sense of the term even though they propound for a greater Assamese nationality.

The plains tribal were also left out from the Sixth Schedule of the Constitution which provides for the establishment of the district councils for hill districts of north eastern region including the state of Assam. These district Councils act as local self government for the benefit of the hill people, levies taxes on them for their revenue, and prevent the influx of outsiders into the hill districts besides preserving their tradition and culture. With regard to Mizoram, Tripura and other states in the north east India the Sixth Schedule was amended by the Lok Sabha in recent years and greater autonomy has been granted to the governments of these states towards the aspirations of the tribal population. However, nothing in this regard has been done for the plains tribes in Assam. The plains tribal of Assam allege that the constitutional discrimination is also evident in the provisions of the Sixth Schedule of the Constitution which sanction the constitution of the state level committees for the economic development and welfare of the tribal people all over India. The differentiation between the hill tribal and the plain tribal Bodo people and the consequent special provisions extended to the hill tribal in the northeast is the root cause of ferment among the Bodos today. It is surprising that despite the Bodos being the largest tribal group in the state, no special constitutional arrangement was considered necessary to ensure a measure of political or at least administrative power to them.

The Bodo dominated area is in the north bank of the River Brahmaputra in the state of Assam. The Bodo movement was started with the objective of achieving a separate province or homeland for the plain tribe Bodo as they are living in the state of Assam since time immemorial. Certainly there is geographical and demographic concentration of tribal people in the area. The proposed area which has been demanded for homeland for the plains Bodos is tribal majority compact area and excludes the non tribal majority area. The proposed Bodoland area has got all feasibility and it satisfies all the criteria for a separate state. It comprises a contiguous area starting from Sonkosh river in the west Bengal-Assam border and on the west to Sadiya and on the East in the north bank of the Brahmaputra of Assam where the plains tribal Bodo people are mostly concentrated.

On the other hand, natural boundary is not an overall necessary factor for creating a separate state which is evident from the existing states. Even, contiguousness is not a rigid factor for the creation of a separate state like Goa and Union Territory like Daman & Diu. As regards area, the proposed Bodoland will have enough area (25,478 sq. km) as well which is much bigger than the area of Meghalaya (22,429 sq. km), Mizoram (21,081 sq. km), Nagaland (16,579 sq. km) and Tripura (10,416 sq. km). In terms of population there were 29 lakhs population in Bodoland Territorial Area District of which tribal population constituted 51.30 per cent and Bodos constituted 80.9 per cent of tribal population whereas Meghalaya was having 23 lakhs population, Mizoram had 8.9 lakhs population only as per 2001 Census were granted statehood. Ironically, Bodoland has been repeatedly denied of such opportunities by some sections of politicians and intellectuals of the country when Bodo population and areas of proposed *Bodoland* have been significantly larger as compared to smaller northeastern states. Thus, judging and analysing elaborately from these points of view there is every justification for the demand and creation of Bodoland within Indian Union. It is generally believe that political self-determination can only be able to bring complete and concrete political as well as all-round security to the plains tribe Bodos in Assam. Alternative to that, nowhere they can feel safe and secured and a separate homeland for tribal community only would be able to make the tribal prosperous and recognisation to the nationalities. The plains tribal of Assam must have to enjoy the internationally accepted principle of right to political self-determination. As such tribal must have a self Govt. in Assam. The view of the leaders are let the Assamese also enjoy the right to political self–determination, survive and prosper in a separate homeland and the plains tribal also must be allowed to survive and prosper in a separate homeland.

It has been examined and considered that the 20th century can be said as an era of uprising of the tribal and down trodden people for the political right of self-determination in the world. At the global level, in every nook and corner, the people have been witnessing the struggle of the tribal and down trodden people for their political, constitutional and human rights. The question of right of self-determination and identity is admitted by the United Nations and the Constitution of India also does not stand against it. Since demand for Bodoland stands for the question of right of self-determination, and their identity assertion it is coherently agreeable that opposition or protection to the demand will mean the opposition or protection to the internationally accepted principle.

The optimistic idea as well as holistic approach and political philosophy of smaller states opined and given by Late Jaiprakash Narayan should be experimented. The smaller states should be made true federating units of India with more autonomy and it would show a path to solve the problems of communal clashes. The small administrative units would help to progress rapidly and there by creation of small administrative units would mean decentralization of powers among federating units, of course, these powers should be governed with a socialistic, political philosophy, and a holistic administrative set-up. Economic structure and legal systems will be much more favorable for solving multifarious problems of the country in a radical manner.

In the recent past, when the Bharatiya Janata Party (BJP) was in power, it openly supported the concept of smaller states and adopted the policy to create three new states, namely, Uttarakhand, Jharkhand and Chattisgarh carving out of Uttar Pradesh, Bihar and Madhya Pradesh respectively. But while implementing the policy to create smaller states they adopted partisan attitude and accordingly the demand for Bodoland was looked down upon as per the wishes of the Chauvinist ruling clique in Assam. This only opened the path of never ending crisis in the region. It is very pertinent to mention that if the U.S.A. by having 51 states can run the country very smoothly and prosperously then why can't India create some more states including Bodoland which would not only provide better administration but would also ensure balanced development among different linguistic groups in the country. This would probably go a long way not only in strengthening the nation but also in fulfilling the aspirations of every sections of the society including various ethnic groups of the country.

Bodo Aspirations in Historical Perspective

Pre-Independence Awareness

It is not easy rather difficult to analyze the position of Bodos during pre-independence period. As we know Bodos are also known as Kacharis the earliest inhabitants of Indo-Mongoloid stock to settle in the Brahmaputra valley and they are the largest group among all other plain tribes of the Brahmaputra valley of Assam. The first ethnographic account of the Bodos of Assam was published by Rev. Endle in 1911 in which they were referred to as Kachari. They were recognized as a scheduled tribe after independence. It is the European scholars like Hodgson (1828) and Grierson (1903) who had used the term *Kachari* and *Bodo* interchangeably to refer to this linguistic group of Assam. Grierson (1903) identified them as Indo-Mongoloid people belonging to the Tibeto-Burman language family. He has further maintained that the generic name *Bodo* was first used by Hodgson to refer a group of languages.

It has been historically observed that prior to the establishment of British rule in India the existence of the Bodos was on the verge of extinction. They were quite unaware of their societal dignity, pride and honour. For centuries, tradition of structural assimilation as a process of social change remained as a popular tradition among the Bodos. The modern civilization installed by the British Govt. in India totally changed the traditional mindset of the Bodos. Under the new liberal intellectual atmosphere set by the British rule, the Bodo people developed the sense of self respect, identity consciousness of their society and soon they started to reassert their community identity by reviewing and restructuring their lost history, culture, tradition, custom, language etc. But during the British rule, many Bodo people merged into Assamese population thereby reducing their statistics in the subsequent census decades even after independence. It was under the British rule the Bodos first raised the demand for a separate electorate roll of Bodo people along with hill tribes of the north-east India. In 1929, the *Kachari Yubak* committee submitted a memorandum to the Simon Commission demanding safeguard which would ensure them an independent identity. Subsequently the formation All Assam Plains Tribal League in 1933 encouraged them and made conscious among tribal communities for their identity assertion in Assam. This consciousness gradually took a definite form and developed to the stage of demanding the development of Bodo language and literature and side by side fully supported statehood demand for Bodoland in order to safeguard the interest of Bodos through political means.

Post-Independence Developments

After Independence, aspirations of Bodos regarding their identity and cultural affiliation got importance with the philosophy of self-realization. Realizing their past history and in order to regain their glorious past which were lost in the 13th century, they tried their hard to mobilize among themselves. They also visualised as they were farmers, peasants and earliest inhabitants of the state. At the beginning, Bodos were on the modern line of education and through their education; they strived hard to educate their generation to come. However, Bodo did not exist their own script for which they had to take education through Assamese script. Among them many writers well recognised through Assamese version. Before the emergence of Bodo Sahitya Sabha (BSS) there exists no influence on Assamese nationality but the emergence of Bodo Sahitya Sabha has created among the Bodos a new revolution on Bodo language and literature. Since the formation, the Sabha worked for the welfare of Bodo society and under its banner it tried to unite all Bodo writers towards developing Bodo language. The Sabha gives a platform to develop Bodo language systematically in written forms and helped the writers to create Bodo literature through its banner. The Sabha has been demanding introduction of Bodo as a medium of instruction ever since its inception. The movement for reassertiveness was started with this sociocultural organization among the Bodos after Independence.

The All Bodo Students Union, the most influential organization campaigning for a separate Bodo homeland, defined the term 'Bodo' as those who speak or are supposed to have one spoken language belonging to the Bodo group. The Bodos are the most important Indo Mongoloid people in Eastern India and they migrated from South-West China to North-East India through Tibet and Bhutan centuries ago. Historically, under colonial rule and also after independence, major sections of Bodos merged into the Assamese population.

In 1967, when Indira Gandhi declared for reorganization of Assam state on a federal basis, the All Bodo Students Union warmly welcomed the statement and since then the Bodos under the banner of All Bodo Students Union have been demanding bifurcation of Assam for the creation of a separate state for the plain tribal of Assam. The political awakening of the Bodos took a new turn on 27th February, 1967 with the formation of a political party, Plains Tribal Council of Assam (PTCA). Ever since its formation with the support of All Bodo Students Union as the largest political party has been demanding a separate Union Territory to be called Udayachal comprising of the Bodo-dominated areas all along the northern bank of the river Brahmaputra extending from the western border of Kokrajhar district right up to the eastern border of North Lakhimpur district (Roy, 1995). However, the demand for Udayachal never materialized. Many political parties came to power, and thus players changed and so did the game. By the end of 70's it became clear that Bodos had a little or no influence in the Indian political process.

In 1968 the Plains Tribal Council of Assam launched a campaign to boycott the General Election, particularly in the Kokrajhar Parliamentary Constituency, which is the only reserve seat for tribal out of the 14 parliamentary seats in the state. In their bid to stop candidate from filing nominations many Bodos were subjected to bullet injuries and police torture. A map of the proposed "Udayachal" state was prepared and a memorandum was submitted to the then President Sri V.V. Giri, Prime Minister Smt Indira Gandhi and also the Home Ministry. All Bodo Students Union with the support of Bodo Sahitya Sabha and other allied Bodo organizations demanded for Bodoland which was the direct legacy of the Plains Tribal Council of Assam movement for Udayachal. The Plain Tribal Council of Assam which initially had the support of the All Bodo Students Union had unsuccessfully pressed the demand during re-organization of the north-eastern region.

Ever since All Bodo Students Union launched its movement on 2nd March 1987, it has completed various phases of its agitation and has been able to mobilize mass support mostly in the Bodo dominated areas. Some Bodo dominated areas like Kokrajhar, Barpeta, Nalbari and Udalguri have become the centre of the militant activities for Bodoland. For exactly ten years now, the Bodos under the banner of All Bodo Students Union has been spearheading what it calls a mass-revolution for a separate homeland and a full-fledged state for the plains Bodos though their original demand as incorporated in their first memorandum to the then Chief Minister of Assam, P.K. Mahanta and former State Governor, Bhishma Narain Singh on 1st January 1987, was a separate homeland with the status of a Union Territory. The Bodo movement initially included 92 demands of many points of vital interests to the Bodos were abandoned in favour of three principal political demands.

Accordingly, the Central Govt. and Govt. of Assam kept their assurance to look into the Bodo issue. The year 1993 witnessed a significant development in the political setup of the Bodos. A historic record known as Bodo Accord was signed on 20th February 1993 and this led the creation of Bodoland Autonomous Council (BAC) with the objective to provide maximum autonomy to the Bodos for their socio-economic, ethnic and cultural advancement of course within the framework of the Constitution.

However, soon after the formation of Bodoland Autonomous Council, both the Governments were urged to finalize the total number of villages to be included under the jurisdiction of Bodoland Autonomous Council and to demarcate the area in consultation with All Bodo Students Union and Bodo People's Action Committee as per the Accord. But trouble arose while identifying such villages having 50 per cent or more population of plain tribe. The Bodo leaders and the State Govt. failed in taking a final decision as no consensus emerged on village-wise population figures on plain tribes under Bodo Autonomous Council. In all 2570 villages situated in a vast and contiguous area extending from the western border of Kokrajhar right up to eastern border of Majbat Constituency of Darrang district were included in the Council area. Since demarcation of contiguous area did not satisfy all the sections of Bodo leaders and many of them took their firm stand and urged both the Governments

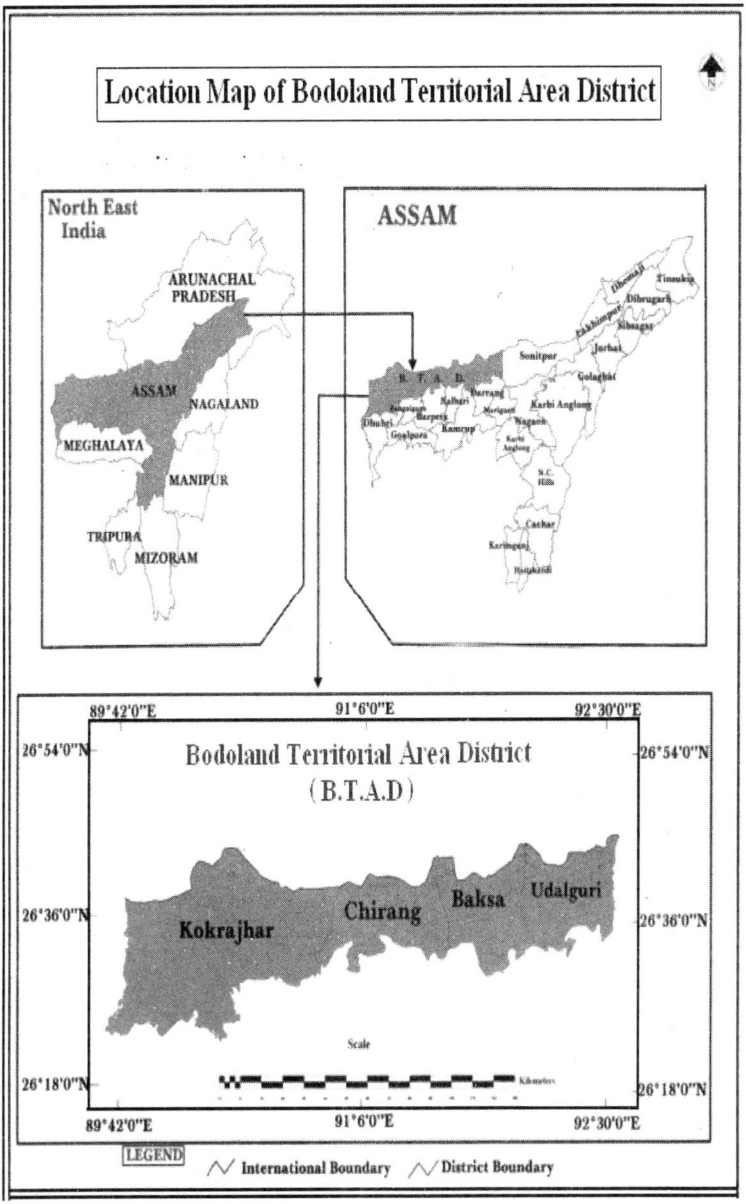

Map 2.1: Bodo Inhabited Districts of Assam

to include five hundred more villages in it. However, the Government did not readily concede their demand but agreed to look into the matter for further consideration. Finally, the Bodo leaders under the banner of All Bodo Students Union and Bodo People's Action Committee adopted a resolution and declared to denounce the first Bodo Accord and resumed the movement with new vigour. The Bodos, particularly All Bodo Students Union volunteers who had surrendered to the government after the signing the first Bodo Accord, some of them formed a militant group, Bodo Liberation Tigers (BLT) in a meeting held at Dotoma in Kokrajhar district on June 18, 1996. Conforming to the political demand of All Bodo Students Union, the extremist group, Bodo Liberation Tigers resolved to adopt an ideology of creating a separate State remaining within the sovereignty of India. The mass people extended their support to Bodo Liberation Tigers in the interest of their ultimate goal, the Bodoland state.

Ultimately after a long 10 years of movement the time came for signing of Bodo Accord-II on 10th February 2003 with which Bodoland Territorial Council (BTC) or Bodoland Territorial Area District (BTAD) comprising all the 3082 villages was created with an amendment under the Sixth Schedule of the Constitution of India.

Conclusion

Obviously, the above analysis shows that political economy of Bodo movement which started as a socio-cultural movement during the last part of the twentieth century emerged not from a single factor but it comprised of many issues with which the movement crystallized. Socio-economic, ethnic identity and cultural heritage, language, etc were the main forces which worked behind the Bodo movement.

Historical aspiration among Bodos was a revolution. The analysis throws light that though Bodos were on the verge of extinction before the establishment of British administration in India. It was British rule in India which totally changed the traditional mindset of the Bodos. It was the British people who encouraged the Bodos to develop the sense of self respect and identity consciousness of their society. Their encouragement helped the Bodos to start to reassert their community identity. It is also found that during British rule, Bodos first raised the demand for a separate entity along with hill tribes of the north-east India. The movement for re-assertiveness was started with this socio-cultural organization among the Bodos after Independence. Accordingly, the emergence of Bodo organizations united Bodo people on language, cultural heritage, and ethnic identity.

3

Outline of the Present Study

This chapter presents a clear picture of the framework designed to carry out our present research study. It narrates the objectives of the study, sets the hypotheses, and discusses the methodology adopted to fulfill the objective and decide about the hypotheses. This chapter also introduces the nature and sources of data used in this study to test the hypothesis.

Objectives

The study is undertaken keeping in mind the following few objectives:

1. To evaluate the human development status of Bodos as compared to the State of Assam.
2. To identify the factors behind Bodo Movement by examining their socio-economic status, drawn from primary sources.
3. To present a descriptive and analytical frame through which the inference can be drawn about the role of the status of human development for the Bodo Movement in Assam.
4. To suggest some inclusive policy measures for avoiding such movements when both national integrity and social fabrics are at stake.

Hypotheses

The study would aim at testing the following hypotheses:

1. Bodos in Assam are systematically lagging behind other sections of population in terms of the expansion in human development.
2. Poor expansion of human development, along with other factors, has played an important role in triggering the Bodo Movement in Assam.

Methodology

Methodology which has been considered a device through which the purpose of the study is achieved is very much necessary. This is required to fulfill our research objectives and to decide about the set hypotheses a specific research methodology needs to be designed. The study has actually the following designed present methodology consists of three distinct parts:

1. Document Reviews
2. Question-Answer Type Interviews
3. Focus Group Discussions.

First, in Document Review taking the stock of secondary information the study attempts to evaluate the status of human development in Bodo-inhabited five districts of Assam as considered or chosen for the study purpose. The status of overall Human Development Index (HDI) and of different dimensions of human development of these districts is empirically measured so that the relative position of these districts in the list of all districts of Assam can be monitored. This analysis will help us to test our first hypothesis.

The second part of our analysis which will decide the fate of the second hypothesis is based on primary information collected from those five districts of Assam and clubbing these districts into four ones which are included in the BTAD. The questionnaire is designed in such a fashion that along with the information of human development indicators the Bodo aspirations on autonomy/statehood can be studied.

Finally, in the third stage of the study Focus Group Discussions (FGD) are conducted to obtain qualitative judgment of the concerned people of different categories.

Data Sources

The Scheme of Data Collection: Data from the secondary sources that would help us to analyze the various socio-economic variables in the study for the development of Bodos along with education as well as human development among Bodos of the study area are not available. The Census data limit themselves to the literate persons, income, expenditure, sex-ratio, mortality rate, student's enrolment in schools both in primary as well as in secondary and occupational distribution of population as workers. Therefore, it has been planned to collect the relevant data through a primary survey, by visiting the households ourselves with a detailed questionnaire. This method of obtaining data has strong as well as weak points of its own. On the one hand, it is not possible for an individual to visit a very large number of households in the villages scattered in a large area and therefore, the sample size must be kept at its modest level. On the other hand, the opportunity given by meeting the households in person provides a great scope for an in-depth investigation. Details on school enrolment, income, expenditure, mortality rate, sex-ratio, income from various sources, consumption-expenditure, family size, etc. can be obtained from such an enterprise.

Selection of Sample: The Bodoland Territorial Area District (BTAD) was created under Sixth Schedule of the Constitution of India in 2003. In Bodoland Territorial Area District there are four districts, namely, Baksa, Chirang,

Kokrajhar and Udalguri. While at the time of creation Bodoland Territorial Area District, major areas of five districts of present Assam namely, Barpeta, Bongaigaon, Darrang, Kokrajhar and Darrang, and in addition, few Bodo inhabited villages from other districts of the state had been included. We have chosen Bodoland Territorial Area District as the focused area of the present study the reason being that sixty per cent villages of all five districts were covered under the jurisdiction of Bodoland Territorial Area District. The administrative unit was created with a mission to accomplish overall development of the area along with socioeconomic, cultural and linguistic aspirations of the Bodo people. Bodoland Territorial Area District was created by taking the then Kokrajhar district, and major parts of Legislative Assembly Constituency (LAC) from the districts of Barpeta, Bongaigaon, Kokrajhar, Darrang and Nalbari and some areas from other districts. More precisely, Bodoland Territorial Area District covers Legislative Assembly Constituency of Sorbhog, Bhabanipur, Patacharkuchi, Barpeta and Chapaguri from Barpeta district; Legislative Assembly Constituency of Sidli, Bongaigaon, Bijni and Abhayapuri from Bongaigaon district; Paneri, Kalaigaon, Sipajhar, Mongaldai, Dalgaon, Udalguri and Mazbat from Darrang district; Tamulpur, Nalbari and Barama from Nalbari district; Gauripur, Golakganj, Bilashipara West and Bilshipara East from Dhubri district; Kamalpur and Rangia from Kamrup district; Barchola from Sonitpur district. After the formation of Bodoland Territorial Area District four districts were renamed as: Kokrajhar, Chirang, Baksa and Udalguri. For administrative purposes the Bodoland Territorial Area District has further been divided into six Sub Divisions namely Portbotjora in Kokrajhar District; Bijni and Kajolgaon in Chirang District; Salbari and Tamulpur in Baksa District; and finally, Bhergaon in Udalguri District. The entire jurisdiction under Bodoland Territorial Area District is presently spread over 25 Development Blocks, 13 Revenue

Circles, 415 Village Council Development Committees (VCDC) and 3082 villages.

The Bodoland Territorial Area District in the state of Assam is bounded by the Himalayan Kingdom of Bhutan in the North, the Brahmaputra River in the South, river Paasnoi in the East and the Sonkosh River in the West. Geographically its boundary lies between 26°18'0" to 26°54'0" N Latitudes and between 89°48'0" E to 92°24'0" E Longitudes and is in the north western part of Assam. It covers 8970 sq. km. of area and is about 11.24 per cent of the total area of the state and is known as the gateway to the northeast India. The total population of Bodoland Territorial Area District area was 2631289 of which 1354629 populations were Scheduled Tribe out of which 1083701 were Bodo populations which accounts 80 per cent and Scheduled Cast populations are 137544 and 1139118 are General population. Here 12 villages have been selected and taking three villages from each District a total of three hundred households were surveyed taking 25 households from each village.

While selecting villages and sampling units the main concern was to ensure variability of data. At the village level a number of factors determine variability, viż. connectivity by road, distance from the township, availability of power or electricity, population size of the village, school enrolment, literacy rate, mortality rate, income, consumption, expenditure, etc. The role of these factors lies in determining the socio economic status and human development of the Bodos in the study area and their relative progressiveness. Connectivity by road and distance from a township influence availability of inputs, disposability of output, consumption pattern, approach to education and information, etc. which, in turn, determine the socioeconomic structure of the village and human development among the Bodo population. These factors also influence living conditions of the people in the area. Availability of power influences productivity along with standard of living and the consumption pattern which determines the quality of life. Today when almost every implement/equipment and durable consumer goods have become electrical and or electronic in nature, unavailability of power in a village seriously jeopardizes its prospects in the spheres of production as well as consumption.

Keeping these considerations in mind, the study planned to select villages some of which are nearer to the towns while others are far away from the town. Since Bodos are more concentrated in the villages which are far away from town, we decided to select one village from each district which is nearer to town and two villages that are far away from town. The study's stand in fixing the number of sample households from each village rests on two considerations. Firstly, it is more concerned with the overall socio-economic structure of the community. Secondly, it is expected that the inter-relationships among different variables in every village are more stable than the values of those variables themselves. A sample of twenty-five households would capture the inherent inter-relationships among different variables and while larger samples are always preferred to smaller samples. Having decided the sample villages and the number of samples to be drawn from each village collection works went ahead to draw random samples from these villages. As mentioned earlier as the study had already enumerated the households in each village with the name of the head of the household in next there arranged the households in an ascending lexicographic order of the name of the heads of households and assigned to them a serial number 1 to N_i. Then, uniformly distributed random numbers lying between 1 and N_i were generated for each village. Here N_i is the total number of households in the village i (i=1,2,...) as found in the enumeration. These random numbers indicated as to which households to survey in each village. Since there cannot be any relationship between the lexicographic ordering of names and the random numbers generated by the study has been holding that every household in a village got an equal chance of being selected.

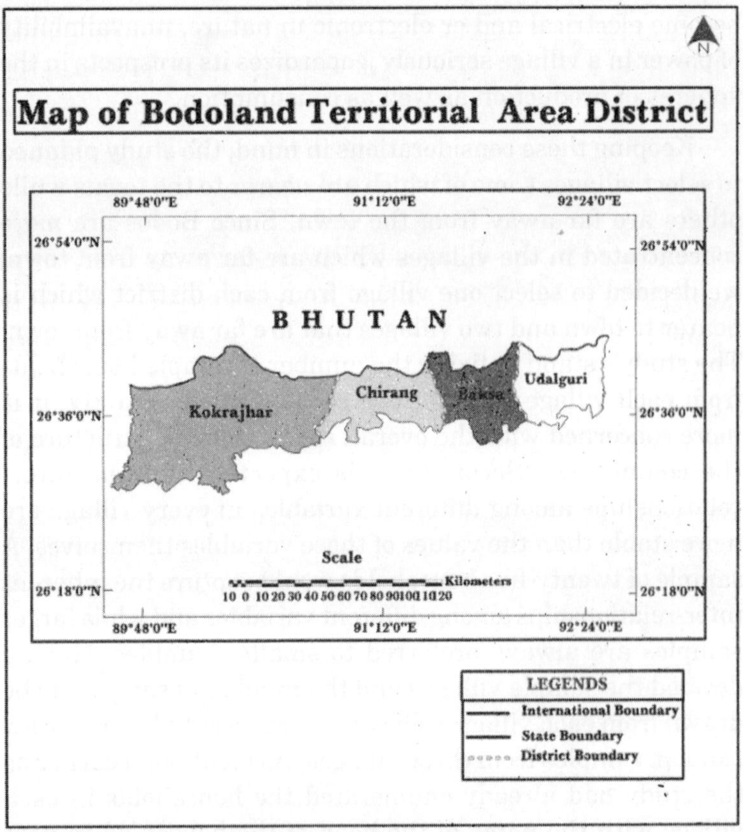

Map 3.1 Study Area

Data Collection: Then there after served a detailed questionnaire to the randomly chosen head of the respective households in each village. In most cases they were to be explained as to what information we needed from them. Sometimes the respondent had to seek assistance of other members of the family to give the information. Normally enumerator could get two to three filled-in questionnaires per day. Every evening, enumerator crosschecked the information for consistency, and in case of some inconsistency, they met the respondents on the subsequent day and removed the inconsistencies. The program of data collection for a village lasted for some 20 days on an average, albeit with intervals of a few days during the span. Occasionally, they could not meet some head of the household. But meeting him on some other day was not a problem. Enumerators could collect data from all the 12 villages in a little over six months. The data collections were conducted during 2003.

Tabulation and Analysis: After collection of data, the same were presented in the form of a table using Microsoft Excel spread sheet. Apart from tabulation and use of descriptive statistics, we used simple statistical, mathematical tools and the most popular method used by the Planning Commission, Govt. of India to estimate various indices of human development such as Human Development Index (HDI), Education Index (EI), Consumption Index (CI) and Health Index (HI), etc.

In the third stage of the research Focus Group Discussions were conducted in each of the sample villages taking ten respondents in each group. The formations of the groups are based on some predetermined criterion which is discussed in detail in the relevant chapter of this study.

4

Bodos: An Introduction

This chapter draws an outline of the present status of human development in Assam with a special reference to Bodo-inhabited districts of the state. First, identity of Bodos has been very briefly introduced and the demographic profile of the state is discussed in such a fashion that the Bodo dominated settlements can be spotted. This section also discusses the population characteristics as well as the demographic transition that had taken place in Assam during 1990s. Next, the socioeconomic profile of the Bodos has been captured from secondary sources. Finally, the present status of human development in the state with special reference to Bodo-inhabited districts is summarized.

Identity of the Bodos

The Kacharis, who are known as the Bodos, are one of the oldest inhabitants of Assam. Many eminent historians claim that in olden days Bodos were living in Mongolia and Siberia and they migrated from there, lived in the Bod country. The Bod country or a place said to have existed between Nepal and Tibet. The inhabitants of Bod country or a living place were called as Bodo, Bodo-Ficha, and Bodosa. Later on they migrated towards the northeastern part of India and settled on the north banks of the river Brahmaputra. After migration, the Bodosa came to be known as Dimasa meaning thereby the children of big river where *Dwi* or *Di* means river and fisa means children. With the passage of time, Dimasa the children of the river were driven out from the banks of the Brahmaputra river towards Sadiya by Pushya Varman of Varman dynasty in the 4th century. Later on they established their new kingdom on the bank of river Dhansiri and built their capital at Dimapur in 1086 AD from which they ruled for over 450 years. In the 13th century, the Ahoms led by Sukapha came to Assam and occupied one portion of the Kachari Kingdom and by 1536 AD; they occupied the entire Kachari kingdom. This forced them to flee towards the North Cachar Hills from Dimapur. In 1536, the Kacharis came to Maibong and ruled till 1750 AD from there and the last Kachari king Gobindra Chandra was assassinated in 1830 AD that brought to an end of Kachari ruled. The Bodos can therefore boast of their glorious cultural history as well and they have distinctive culture, tradition, language and literature of their own. In the opinion of many scholars the Mongolian culture began to influence the Aryan culture with inter marriage system during that period. With passage of time Bodos became weak in number and scattered here and there, forgot their own language and culture. Thus, Bodos can sustain from cultural and linguistic onslaught of developed neighbor communities as they love their mother tongue, they preserved their rich culture and tradition in origin and absolute form.

In the opinion of many scholars the Bodo is a generic term which includes the Boro-Kachari, the Mech-Kachari etc. The Bodo or Boro has been interchangeably used by the writers ever since the publication of the works of Brian Hodgson (1912). Hodgson was the author to confer the generic name on the tribe and other cognate tribes belonging to the same linguistic family. According to Grierson (1903) generic name Bodo was first used by Hodgson to this group of languages. Endle (1911) in his introductory chapter of the monograph incorporated in the census report of 1881 notes that the said linguistic group attaches great importance to the word Bodo-Fisha or Bodosa by which they call themselves. He noted that they were known as the kachris to others and Boro to themselves. Scholars like Grierson, Endle and others have favored the term Bara, Baro and Bodo as the national name of the community. According to Anderson it is a name given to the Tibetan-Burman linguistic group by the Hindus. Gait views the term Kachari as derived from a Sanskrit word which means bordering region. He also adds that the district of Cachar might have got its name directly from this word or it might have been so called after its principal tribe. According to Bordoloi (1984) the term Kachari is used to denote a good number of tribal communities originally belonging to the same stock of population such as the Bodo-Kachari, Dimacha-Kachari, and Mech-Kachari etc. Bordoloi in his monograph 1984 holds the view that as the opinions of scholar vary in regard to the term Kachari it can be presumed that term is used by the outsiders to designate some ethnic tribal communities belonging to the Bodo group. Edward gait also holds the view that the name Kachari was given by the outsiders and to him in the Brahmaputra valley the Kacharis call themselves Bodo-Fisha or Bodosa as sons of the Bodos. Recently, All Bodo Students union and leaders prefer to call themselves as Bodo the common generic name as known to every Bodo people in the world.

Origin and Settlement of Bodos

The state of Assam was the meeting ground for diverse races and tribes. Streams of human races and tribe of Austro-Asiatic, Negritos, Dravidians, Alpines, Indo-Mongoloids, Tibet-Burman and Aryans penetrated into Assam through different routes and contributed in their own way towards the unique fusion of a new community which came to be known as

Assamese to the world. The Tibeto-Burmans are the predominant group in the whole of Assam and among them the Bodos are the largest in number.

There is no historical record as regards the origin and migration of the Bodos. The original homeland of the speakers of the Tibeto-Burman language is said to be in the north-west china from where they migrated and the group became diversified somewhere in north-Burma, with one group migrating westward along the sub-Himalayan, entered the Brahmaputra valley by the north-eastern route while another group moved southwards to reach as far as south-east Asia. These different groups later on entered the north-east India through different routes. The Bodos or Kacharis claim to have migrated to the Brahmaputra valley from central Asia at around 5000 BC and according to Gait (1981) it is an accepted fact that the Kacharis entered into the Brahmaputra valley much before the Indo-Aryans. Certain legends are prevalent among some Bodo tribes regarding their origin and migration. Playfair (1909) in his monograph elaborately deals with the migratory routes of the Garo from their ancestral homeland Tibet to their present habitat the Garo Hills. In the opinion of Endle (1911) Bodo population has been found both in north and south of Brahmaputra valley and the legends of Garo and Rabha are the testimony to the fact that the ancestors of the Bodos crossed Brahmaputra to reach its southern bank where the Garo are presently settled. Another section migrated further south and east to take the name Dimasa while third group moved further south-west to tripura and adjoining areas where they are known as hill tripura. Further the group inhabiting the Nowgaon district is known as Lalung and their eastern expansion brought about some sections of the Kacharis like sonowal, thengal sonowal etc where some of the Kacharis, Rabha, Mech and others who were left behind now occupy different places of the northern bank of Brahmaputra.

As regards the early history of the Kacharis, Soppit (1885) views that the legends would lead one to contend that the race originally inhabited the hills and slopes to the north of the Brahmaputra and then gradually extended through central Assam to mymensing district and on being gradually driven into upper Assam from Guwahati the king established himself at Dimapur. According to him, the Dimasa Kachari of the north Cachar hills still believe that they once ruled in kamrupa and their royal family traced its descent from the kings of that kingdom. In view of the extension of the Bodo language Chatterjee (1974) opines that Bodos appear to have settled first over the entire Brahmaputra valley and latter extended towards north Bengal. He adds that the Indo-Mongoloid who penetrated into north Bihar might have been Bodos. In southern bank of Brahmaputra they occupied Garo Hills from where they further spread southward to northern mymensing where the semi-Bengalised Hajong tribe is of Bodo origin. In Assam from Nowgaon they extended to Cachar district and into syllet. According to Chatterjee the Bodos spread over the whole of the Brahmaputra valley and north Bengal as well the then east Bengal forming a solid block of Indo-Mongoloid people in eastern India.

Demographic Profile of Bodos in Assam

Assam is one of the most ethnically diverse states in the country. A number of ethnic groups are living in the state. Table 4.1 depicts that total tribal population in the state, according to the Census of India 2001, has been recorded as 33,08,570 accounting for 12.41 per cent of state population. The decadal growth rate of tribal population in the state is estimated as 15.15 per cent as compared to 18.92 per cent of total state population growth. Among the main tribes of Assam, Bodos and Miris together account for roughly half of the total tribal population of the state. Bodos alone constitute about 41 per cent of the total tribal population, followed by Miris with 18 per cent, Karbis with 11 per cent and Sonowal Kacharis with 7 per cent.

The spread of tribal population across the districts of Assam is, however, not even. The Bodos, the tribe of our concern, are mostly concentrated in five Districts of Assam namely, Barpeta, Bongaigaon, Darrang, Kokrajhar and Nalbari. In these five districts total Bodo population in 1991 was 7.15 lakhs, account for about 13.43 per cent of the total population of these districts. After a decade in 2001 the Bodo population increased to 8.42 lakhs, accounting for 13.73 per cent of the total population.

Table 4.1
Tribal population in Assam 2001

Tribe	*Population*		*Per Cent of Total Tribal Population of the State*	
	1991	*2001*	*1991*	*2001*
Bodo	11,84,569	13,52,771	41.12	40.9
Miri	3,81,562	5,87,310	13.27	17.8
Karbi	3,55,032	3,53,513	12.35	10.7
Rabha	1,35,905	2,77,517	4.73	8.4
Sonowal Kachari	1,14,779	2,35,881	3.99	7.1
Lalung	1,12,424	1,70,622	3.91	5.2
Dimasa	84,654	1,10,976	2.95	3.4
Deori	32,633	41,161	1.14	1.2
Others	4,72,863	1,78,819	16.45	5.3
Total Tribal Population	28,74,421	33,08,570	100	100
Total State Population	2,24,14,322	2,66,55,528	–	–

Source: Census of India, 1991 & 2001.

Assam accounts for about 2.4 per cent of the country's geographical area and its 26.84 million people are 2.59 per cent of the country's population and Table 4.2 depicts the area of respective districts in the state. Bodo inhabited five districts had 14673 sq. km area in 2001, accounting for roughly 23 per cent of the total geographical area of the state. The density of population in five districts was recorded as 364 in 1991 which increased to 416 per sq. km in 2001; with the corresponding figures for the state of 286 in 1991 and 340 in 2001. Therefore, it reveals that the population density in our concerned five districts is considerably higher than the state average. This also indicates that almost Bodo people are living in villages and low level of development and low trend of urbanization in the concerned area are the most accountable factors for being the area of the higher density of population in the concern area. Sex-ratio is taken as an important indicator of population which is a measure of number of females per thousand of male population. As far as sex-ratio is concerned, Bodo inhabited districts had continuously higher sex-ratio against the state average. However, sex ratio in different districts cf Assam as well as among the Bodo inhabited districts of the state is not satisfactory. This is basically because of two reasons as found to be noted. First, the state has patriarchal society which did allow discrimination between a daughter and a son. Second, in Assam since women were not received education and proper healthcare their survival chances were not as good as those of males. Sex selective abortions were possible in a patriarchal society and thus sex ratio in Assam has not been by and large determined by the biological strength of the females. Further, poor economic condition reflects adverse sex ratio. In fact, since Assam being the state of predominance of agriculture easily explains the preference for sons because when they grow they provide agricultural labour for cultivations. Since over the years nothing has happened to

Table 4.2
Demographic profile of Assam

District	*Area*	*1991*			*2001*		
	(Sq. Km)	*Population*	*Density*	*Sex Ratio*	*Population*	*Density*	*Sex Ratio*
1	*2*	*3*	*4*	*5*	*6*	*7*	*8*
Barpeta	3245	1385658	247	939	1647201	508	941
Bongaigaon	2152	807523	322	940	904835	420	945
Darrang	3481	1298860	373	938	1504320	432	944
Kokrajhar	3538	808730	258	940	905764	256	943
Nalbari	2257	1016390	450	936	1148824	509	939
Sub-Total	14673	5317131	364	939	6110944	416	942
Cachar	3786	1215385	321	932	1444921	382	945
Dhemaji	3237	478830	148	927	571944	177	941
Dhubri	2798	1324404	473	950	1637344	585	947
Dibrugarh	3381	1042457	308	905	1185072	351	931
Goalpara	1824	668138	366	947	822035	451	956

(Contd...)

1	*2*	*3*	*4*	*5*	*6*	*7*	*8*
Golaghat	3502	828096	236	920	946279	270	930
Hailakandi	1327	449048	338	929	542872	409	935
Jorhat	2851	871206	306	913	999221	350	933
Kamrup	4345	2000071	460	879	2522324	581	901
K. Anglong	10434	662723	64	907	813311	78	926
Karimganj	1809	827063	457	946	1007976	557	947
Lakhimpur	2277	751517	330	931	889010	390	951
Morigaon	1551	639682	375	941	776256	500	946
Nagaon	3973	1893171	494	929	2314629	582	944
NC Hills	4888	150801	31	857	188079	38	884
Sibsagar	2668	907983	340	907	1051736	394	928
Sonitpur	5324	1424287	288	912	1681513	316	929
Tinsukia	3790	962298	254	891	1150062	303	913
Sub-Total	63765	17097161	268	918	20544584	322	933
All Assam	78438	22414322	286	922	26655528	340	935

Source: Census of India 1991 & 2001.

change the attitude of the people in respect of their preference for sons and there is little possibility of a sustained rise in the female male ratio (FMR) in the state. Poor and illiteracy coupled the situation in terms of male female ratio.

The analysis of the population break up according to age shows an encouraging trend. The proportion of girl children in the age group 0-6 years is more equitable in Bodo inhabited districts than in Assam as a whole, and this has positive implications for the sex ratio in the future. The most densely populated district, Nowgaon has a population density almost sixteen times that of the least densely populated district. Most people in Assam in fact seven of every eight people live in rural areas. In the two decades during 1991 and 2001, there were 935 women for every 1000 men in the state compared to 933 per 1000 for the country. Significantly, there was improvement in sex ratio in Assam but improvement was slightly more in the concerned area interns of sex ratio. This is an extremely positive development.

Table 4.3 gives an idea of population composition of Tribal and Bodo population along with the total population in the districts of Assam for the census year 1991. The share of tribal population varies significantly across the districts of Assam. The highest share of tribal population is recorded in North Cachar Hills District with over 65 per cent of tribal population, followed by Karbi Anglong with 51.56 per cent, Dhemaji with 43.93 per cent. In case of population density and sex ratio are concern the five Bodo inhabited districts show more favorable than the corresponding figures of the state.

High concentration of tribal population in the list of five Bodo-inhabited districts is found in Kokrajhar with 41.15 per cent of tribal population. Similarly, about 32 per cent Bodo Population was recorded in Kokrajhar, followed by Nalbari as of 13 per cent, and Darang by 12 per cent. The

Table 4.3
Population characteristics 1991

District	*Total Population*	*Tribal population*	*% of Tribal to Total Population*	*Bodo Population*	*% of Bodo to Total population*	*% of Bodo to Total Tribal Population*
1	*2*	*3*	*4*	*5*	*6*	*7*
Barpeta	1385658	110452	7.97	90484	6.53	81.92
Bongaigaon	807523	141542	17.53	79541	9.85	56.20
Darrang	1298860	224957	17.32	155863	12.00	69.29
Kokrajhar	808730	329461	41.15	257079	31.78	78.03
Nalbari	1016390	179641	17.67	131623	12.95	73.27
Sub-Total	5317161	986053	18.54	714590	13.43	72.47
Cachar	1215385	16563	1.36	113	0.01	0.68
Dhemaji	478830	210312	43.92	42951	8.97	20.42
Dhubri	1324404	32260	2.42	7080	0.53	21.95
Dibrugarh	1042457	82920	7.95	116	0.01	0.14
Goalpara	668138	115099	17.23	39639	5.93	34.44

(Contd...)

1	2	3	4	5	6	7
Golaghat	828096	84916	10.25	260	0.03	0.30
Hailakandi	449048	715	0.16	—	—	—
Jorhat	871206	105307	12.09	10	—	0.01
Kamrup	2000071	214340	10.72	42740	2.14	19.94
K. Anglong	662723	341718	51.56	86849	13.10	25.42
Karimganj	827063	1430	0.17	—	—	—
Lakhimpur	751517	177156	23.57	117688	15.66	66.43
Morigaon	639682	98483	15.40	385	0.06	0.39
Nagaon	1893171	69848	3.69	218	0.01	0.31
NC Hills	150801	98834	65.54	2143	1.42	2.17
Sibsagar	907983	34496	3.80	87	0.01	0.25
Sonitpur	1424287	152498	10.71	78336	5.50	51.37
Tinsukia	962298	51473	5.35	30	—	0.05
Sub-Total	17097160	1888368	11.04	418645	2.45	22.17
State Average	22414322	2874421	12.82	1133235	5.05	41.12

Source: Census Report 1991, Govt. of India. Souvenir of BSS & ABSU various Issues, Statistical Hand Book, 2001-Assam.

Table 4.4

Population characteristics 2001

District	*Total Population*	*Tribal population*	*% of Tribal to Total Population*	*Bodo Population*	*% of Bodo to Total population*	*% of Bodo to Total Tribal Population*
1	*2*	*3*	*4*	*5*	*6*	*7*
Barpeta	1647201	123266	7.48	109953	6.68	89.20
Bongaigaon	904835	110696	12.23	94435	10.44	85.31
Darrang	1504320	249861	16.61	188520	12.53	75.45
Kokrajhar	905764	304985	34.00	290132	32.03	95.13
Nalbari	1148824	202577	17.63	159448	13.88	78.71
Sub-Total	6110944	991385	16.22	842488	13.73	84.98
Cachar	1444921	18631	1.29	140	0.01	0.75
Dhemaji	571944	270496	47.29	52095	9.11	19.26
Dhubri	1637344	32523	1.98	8781	0.54	27.00
Dibrugarh	1185072	88337	7.45	144	0.01	0.16

(Contd...)

1	*2*	*3*	*4*	*5*	*6*	*7*
Goalpara	822035	131800	16.03	49161	5.98	37.30
Golaghat	946279	93920	9.93	285	0.03	0.30
Jorhat	999221	123134	12.34	12	—	0.01
Kamrup	2522324	250393	9.93	53008	2.10	21.17
K. Anglong	813311	452963	55.69	107676	13.24	23.77
Lakhimpur	889010	308864	23.49	141305	15.89	45.75
Morigaon	776256	120730	15.55	478	0.06	0.40
Nagaon	2314629	89394	3.86	270	0.01	0.30
NC Hills	188079	128428	68.28	2658	1.41	2.07
Sibsagar	1051736	41533	7.95	108	0.01	0.26
Sonitpur	1681513	195083	11.60	94128	5.60	48.25
Tinsukia	1150062	67234	5.85	37	—	0.05
Sub-Total	20544584	2417185	11.76	510286	2.48	21.11
State Average	26655528	3308570	12.41	1352771	5.08	40.89

Source: Census Report 2001, Govt. of India, ABSU, Souvenir of BSS & ABSU, various Issues, Statistical Hand Book-2007-Assam.

sub-total of five Bodo inhabited districts reveal that Bodos comprise about 13.43 per cent of total population in five districts as compared to over 18 per cent of total tribal population.

Tables 4.3 and 4.4 summarize the spread of Bodo as well as total tribal population in the districts of Assam for 1991 and 2001 respectively. As we mentioned earlier that Bodos are mainly concentrated in five districts of Assam, both tables are designed accordingly so that the sub-total, average and other information can be read easily. The upper parts of the tables depict the information and summary of information of the Bodo-inhabited districts while the lower parts depict the information of other districts. Finally, the state level information along with the state averages in the relevant indicators is provided in the last column of the table.

Table 4.4 depicts the identical scenario for 2001. However, it is mention worthy that between two census years (1991 and 2001) the state witnessed massive violence as part of Bodo movement which had a significant impact on the demographic composition of the state especially in the Bodo inhabited five districts. According to an official estimate about 70,000 tribal populations had displaced from these five districts to other parts of the state. As a result the share of tribal population in five Bodo-inhabited districts of Assam has come down to 16.22 per cent of the total population. Similarly, the per cent share of Bodo Population come down to 13.73 per cent, although there has been a marginal increase in the share of total Bodo population in the state during 1990s.

Table-4.5 depicts demographic and health indicators both in Bodo inhabited districts and other districts of Assam. Decadal growth rate (DGR) in Bodo inhabited five districts was recorded 14.71 with the corresponding figure for the state of 18.67 during 1991-2001. The decadal growth rate in our

Table 4.5
Demographic and health indicators

District	*DGR (1991-2001)*	*Urban Population*	*Population aged 65 & above*	*Population below 15 years*
Barpeta	18.53	7.62	5.04	42.3
Bongaigaon	12.23	12.17	4.39	42.4
Darrang	15.79	4.91	4.59	41.1
Kokrajhar	15.05	6.84	4.20	40.8
Nalbari	11.99	2.41	4.80	39.5
Sub Total	14.71	6.79	4.60	41.22
Cachar	18.66	13.97	5.25	38.00
Dhemaji	18.93	6.91	4.15	45.10
Dhubri	23.42	11.66	4.34	44.30
Dibrugarh	12.43	18.77	4.25	37.20
Goalpara	23.07	8.18	4.04	43.4
Golaghat	14.21	8.37	3.94	40.10
Hailakandi	20.92	8.39	4.87	40.4
Jorhat	15.84	16.91	4.45	36.4
Kamrup	25.75	35.81	3.81	37.00
K. Anglong	22.57	11.42	4.20	42.0
Lakhimpur	18.34	7.32	4.46	41.6
Morigaon	21.29	4.91	4.70	43.0
Nagaon	22.30	12.00	4.92	41.2
NC Hills	23.47	31.91	3.24	38.7
Sibsagar	15.95	9.22	4.51	36.6
Sonitpur	17.80	8.81	4.28	39.6
Tinsukia	19.52	19.49	3.92	39.3
Sub Total	19.77	13.41	4.38	40.20
State Average	18.67	11.10	5.49	41.71

Source: Assam Human Development Report, 2003.

concerned five districts is considerably lesser than other districts as well as state average. Census report 2001 shows that urban population in Bodo inhabited districts was recorded as low as of 6.79 per cent with the corresponding figure for 13.41 per cent in other districts and 11.10 per cent as the state average respectively. During 1990s population below fifteen years of age was 41.22 per cent in Bodo inhabited districts while the same was 40.20 per cent in other district of the state with the corresponding figure 41.71 per cent as the state average. Population above sixty five years of age which are also not considered as the workforce constitutes 4.22 per cent in our concerned area whereas the state average is of 5.69 per cent in 2001. This analysis indicates that both children and old persons which were not considered as working population are found less in number in Bodo inhabited district than the state average. In other words, the dependency ratio has been found more among different districts than our concerned area in the state of Assam. It is now seen that over all scenario in many respects in our concerned area displays lagging behind than other districts in the state and the state as a whole.

Table 4.6 categorically relates population characteristics both in Bodo inhabited districts and other districts in Assam. Decadal growth of population in Bodo inhabited five districts in Assam was recorded 15.48 per cent with a corresponding figure for the whole state of 16.93 per cent during the period between 2001 and 2011. The decadal growth of population in the concerned five Bodo inhabited districts is found slightly lesser than the state figure. The table also points out that decadal growth of population in urban areas both in Bodo inhabited districts and in the state is relatively higher than the rural areas. However, the share of rural population varies significantly across the districts of Assam. The highest share of rural population is recorded in Dhubri district with over 27 per cent, followed by Bongaigaon with 22.57 per cent, Dhemaji with 22.51 per cent. The share of rural population is found only 6.79 per cent in Bodo inhabited districts while the corresponding figure was 11.10 per cent in the state with 13.41 per cent in other districts of the state.

Table 4.6
Population characteristics 2011

District	*Total population*			*Percentage Decadal Growth of Population (2001-2011)*		
	Total	*Rural*	*Urban*	*Total*	*Rural*	*Urban*
Kokrajhar	886999	832249	54750	5.19	5.12	6.31
Barpeta	1693190	1545901	147289	21.40	21.93	16.10
Bongaigaon	732639	631813	100826	19.58	22.57	3.72
Darrang	908090	852692	55398	19.51	18.73	32.84
Nalbari	769919	687368	82551	11.74	3.90	200.34
Sub Total	4990837	4550023	440814	15.48	14.45	51.86
Dhubri	1948632	1746715	201917	24.40	27.13	4.92
Goalpara	1008959	871132	137827	22.74	15.36	106.01
Morigaon	957853	884557	73296	23.39	19.82	92.95
Sonitpur	1925975	1754835	171140	15.67	17.83	-2.65
Lakhimpur	1040644	949348	91296	17.06	15.23	40.13
Dhemaji	688077	639605	48472	20.30	19.98	24.82
Tinsukia	1316948	1053956	262992	14.51	13.81	17.43
Dibrugarh	1327748	1083984	243764	12.04	13.31	6.71
Sibsagar	1150253	1040376	109877	9.37	8.99	13.07
Jorhat	1091295	871730	219565	9.21	5.29	28.16
Golaghat	1058674	960892	97782	11.88	11.07	20.51
Karbi Anglong	965280	851158	114122	18.69	17.99	24.14
Dima Hasao	213529	152302	61227	13.53	18.39	3.02
Cachar	1736319	1420309	316010	20.17	14.22	56.92
Karimganj	1217002	1106745	110257	20.74	18.48	49.30
Hailakandi	659260	611087	48173	21.44	22.51	9.27
Kamrup	1517202	1375188	142014	15.67	9.70	144.51
Sub Total	26178435	22230493	3947942	17.38	16.11	37.31
All Assam	31169272	26780516	4388756	16.93	15.35	27.61

Source: Census of India 2011

Socioeconomic Profile of Bodos in Assam

Literacy

Literacy may be regarded as an important instrument to reflect the progress, at the level of understanding in everyday life of individuals. Literacy provides access to knowledge and accelerates the understanding of skills. Therefore, increase in literacy means increase in socio-economic development. According to census reports; the per centage of literate persons in the state as per 1991 census was 52.89 per cent. The per centage of female literate persons in Assam was 34.29 per cent while that of male was 49.98 per cent in the same period. However, it may be mentioned that literacy rate of female went up to 54.61 per cent and that of male had increased to 71.28 per cent in the state and total literacy rate had increased to 63.25 per cent holding 25th position in terms of overall literacy among all States and Union Territories of India.

The Table 4.7 compares the literacy trends of five concerned districts and the other districts of the state for the two successive census years of 1991 and 2001. Lowest literacy rate of 40.47 per cent was observed in Kokrajhar district as against the highest literacy rate of 55.99 per cent in Nalbari in Bodo inhabited districts which was the only districts having higher literacy rate than the state average. The male literacy rate was 39.79 per cent in Kokrajhar which was the lowest among the districts in Bodo inhabited districts and male literacy was highest 54.68 per cent in Nalbari district. Female literacy in the Bodo inhabited districts was only 24.59 per cent which was the lowest among the districts in Bodo inhabited districts and female literacy was highest of 35.83 per cent in Nalbari. However, there was a literacy gap of 30.09 per cent between male and female in Bodo inhabited districts. Nalbari district shows literacy gap between male and female of (18.85 per cent), followed by Bongaigaon (16.15

per cent), Kokrajhar (15.20), Barpeta (15.19 per cent), then by, Darrang (14.87 per cent).

Table 4.7
Literacy trends

	1991			*2001*		
District	*Male*	*Female*	*Total*	*Male*	*Female*	*Total*
Barpeta	41.55	26.36	43.24	64.83	47.07	56.24
Bongaigaon	46.43	30.28	49.06	67.67	50.44	59.33
Darrang	40.71	25.84	42.00	63.91	46.40	55.44
Kokrajhar	39.79	24.59	40.47	60.32	42.40	51.63
Nalbari	54.68	35.83	55.99	76.56	57.26	67.23
Sub-Total	44.44	28.44	45.92	66.00	48.50	57.82
Cachar	56.44	39.55	59.16	75.73	59.41	67.82
Dhemaji	51.08	31.55	53.84	74.41	53.51	64.48
Dhubri	36.45	21.95	38.36	55.91	40.04	48.21
Dibrugarh	55.31	39.92	58.32	77.30	59.95	68.96
Goalpara	40.09	28.93	46.81	64.86	50.85	58.03
Golaghat	54.33	40.00	58.54	77.14	60.99	69.38
Hailakandi	51.78	32.47	53.07	68.24	50.46	59.64
Jorhat	61.66	47.25	65.51	83.62	68.49	76.33
Kamrup	61.47	44.95	65.04	81.16	66.31	74.16
K. Anglong	44.15	26.76	45.57	67.22	47.30	57.70
Karimganj	51.79	35.87	54.71	74.69	57.28	66.24
Lakhimpur	54.86	38.82	58.96	77.06	59.59	68.56
Morigaon	38.05	30.40	47.99	65.15	51.51	58.53
Nagaon	49.84	36.48	54.74	68.27	54.74	61.73
NC Hills	54.39	37.46	57.76	75.67	58.39	67.62
Sibsagar	60.19	46.30	64.46	81.53	66.81	74.47
Sonitpur	46.16	30.90	48.14	67.54	49.73	59.00
Tinsukia	48.26	31.90	50.28	70.15	50.78	60.95
Sub-Total	51.52	36.73	54.99	72.57	55.58	64.68
State Average	49.98	34.29	52.89	71.28	54.61	63.25

Source: Census of India 1991 & 2001.

In 2001, the state literacy rate further has increased to 63.25 per cent leaving the same behind for Bodo inhabited districts to 57.82 per cent. This has shown that during the decade of 1990s, the literacy rate in the state has increased by 10.36 per cent while literacy rate has increased by 11.90 per cent in Bodo inhabited districts. This indicates that literacy rate has increased more in the Bodo inhabited districts than other districts in the state. However, in the case of female literacy rate it was not so significant in the state of Assam. Though there has been a steady increase in the literacy rate for males and females yet the gap has not declined between male and female literacy in every successive census. Female literacy rate in the state was 34.28 per cent in 1991 which was increased to 54.61 per cent in 2001. On the other hand, female literacy rate in Bodo inhabited districts was recorded 28.44 per cent and 48.50 per cent respectively during the same decades. There were many reasons for low level literacy rate in Bodo inhabited districts, particularly among female section.

About 61.87 per cent literacy is recorded for the total tribal population in Bodo inhabited districts against the overall literacy rate of 57.82 per cent as per 2001 census in the state as shown in table-4.8. Tribal Literacy rate in Bodo inhabited districts is ranging from 57.49 per cent in Bongaigaon to 63.08 per cent in Darrang. However, total literacy rate in Bodo inhabited districts ranges from 51.63 per cent to 67.23 per cent and the highest was found in Nalbari (67.23) per cent and the lowest (51.63) per cent in Kokrajhar among the Bodo inhabited five districts. Other districts performed better in terms of tribal literacy of 62.00 per cent than our concerned districts. Among the Bodo inhabited five districts, the highest female tribal literacy rate was found 53.38 per cent in Darrang district and the lowest was 47.71 per cent in Kokrajhar district.

Table 4.8
Literacy rate, 2001

	Literacy Rate Scheduled Tribe Population			*Literacy Rate Total State Population*		
District	*Male*	*Female*	*Total*	*Male*	*Female*	*Total*
Barpeta	73.19	48.70	60.87	64.83	47.07	56.24
Bongaigaon	72.91	52.51	62.69	67.67	50.44	59.33
Darrang	72.58	53.38	63.08	63.91	46.40	55.44
Kokrajhar	67.12	47.71	57.49	60.32	42.40	51.63
Nalbari	71.82	48.54	60.25	76.56	57.26	67.23
Sub Average	71.52	50.57	61.87	66.00	48.50	57.82
Cachar	81.45	71.78	76.60	75.73	59.41	67.82
Dhemaji	70.70	48.79	59.99	74.41	53.51	64.48
Dhubri	77.53	56.20	66.86	55.91	40.04	48.21
Dibrugarh	91.99	79.19	85.64	77.30	59.95	68.96
Goalpara	81.74	64.79	73.27	64.86	50.85	58.03
Golaghat	74.81	53.21	64.30	77.14	60.99	69.38
Jorhat	79.39	60.07	69.88	83.62	68.49	76.33
K. Anglong	64.39	44.67	54.74	67.22	47.30	57.70
Lakhimpur	73.37	51.22	62.48	77.06	59.59	68.56
Morigaon	71.31	50.17	60.77	65.15	51.51	58.53
Nagaon	72.57	54.53	63.66	68.27	54.74	61.73
NC Hills	71.26	53.49	62.63	75.67	58.39	67.62
Sibsagar	83.42	64.07	73.88	81.53	66.81	74.47
Sonitpur	64.47	44.99	54.96	67.54	49.73	59.00
Tinsukia	81.50	65.54	73.80	70.15	50.78	60.95
Sub Average	68.48	47.44	62.00	72.57	55.58	64.68
State Average	72.34	52.44	62.52	71.28	54.61	63.25

Source: Census Report - 2001, Govt. of India.

Table 4.9 depicts literacy trends among scheduled tribes in the state. Literacy rate among Bodos was 41.15 per cent in 1991 which was increased to 51.48 per cent in 2001. Bodo as the major tribe in the state is still lagging behind in terms of literacy rate. This has been observed from table-4.9 and other tribes like Sonowal Kachari, Rabha are on the way leading faster than Bodos in terms of literacy rate. Total tribal literacy rate which was 53.78 per cent in 1991 in the State has increased to 62.52 per cent in 2001.

Table 4.9
Literacy trends among scheduled tribes in Assam

Tribe	*1991*			*2001*			*Improvement During 1990s (By Per cent Points)*
	Male	*Female*	*Person*	*Male*	*Female*	*Person*	
Bodo	49.77	32.53	41.15	59.81	43.00	51.48	10.33
Miri	48.46	28.98	38.72	58.42	39.43	49.12	10.4
Karbi	50.73	33.17	40.35	51.25	34.31	51.25	10.9
Rabha	55.95	32.01	44.98	64.33	48.20	56.37	11.39
S. Kachari	62.60	50.62	56.11	76.22	64.66	70.52	14.41
Lalung	50.33	32.65	41.49	59.77	43.17	51.53	10.04
Dimasa	59.41	36.76	47.04	57.28	40.58	49.14	2.10
Deori	61.68	44.04	52.88	72.72	58.03	65.46	12.58
Others	53.43	45.51	49.47	58.27	42.20	50.54	1.07
State	61.24	46.32	53.78	72.30	52.40	62.52	8.74

Source: Census of India 1991 & 2001 Souvenir of BSS & ABSU, various issues.

Census report 2011 shows information on literacy rate in the irrespective districts of the State. Total literacy rate is found 69.31 per cent in Bodo inhabited district where the same was recorded 74.41 in other districts of Assam with the corresponding figure of 73.18 per cent as the state average.

Table 4.10
Literacy rate in Assam 2011

District	*Literates Persons*			*Literacy Rates*		
	Total	*Rural*	*Urban*	*Total*	*Rural*	*Urban*
Kokrajhar	503178	459155	44023	66.63	65.07	88.85
Barpeta	918708	802463	116245	65.03	62.72	87.22
Nalbari	542680	473689	68991	79.89	78.44	91.46
Bongaigaon	435922	356376	79546	70.44	67.48	87.67
Darrang	489559	456046	33513	64.55	64.38	66.86
Sub Total	2890047	2547729	342318	69.31	67.62	84.41
Dhubri	943680	796343	147337	59.36	56.49	81.83
Goalpara	579038	486547	92491	68.67	67.2	77.64
Morigaon	554143	498740	55403	69.37	67.96	85.35
Nagaon	1755838	1461302	294536	73.78	71.3	89.16
Sonitpur	1160527	1021634	138893	69.96	67.94	89.64
Lakhimpur	697526	626219	71307	78.39	77.45	87.8
Dhemaji	406388	370205	36183	69.07	67.87	84.36
Tinsukia	809796	598332	211464	70.92	66.16	89.03
Dibrugarh	893908	693388	200520	76.22	72.94	90.24
Sibsagar	826951	735534	91417	81.36	80.21	91.99
Jorhat	812328	629728	182600	83.42	81.36	91.39
Golaghat	728513	646433	82080	78.31	76.81	92.54
Karbi Anglong	574509	484646	89863	73.52	71.28	88.53
Dima Hasao	143585	92978	50607	78.99	73.01	92.98
Cachar	1196892	942317	254575	80.36	78.14	89.77
Karimganj	808165	715667	92498	79.72	78.24	93.31
Hailakandi	413705	372302	41403	75.26	73.58	94.67
Kamrup	962677	847747	114930	72.81	71.09	88.65
Sub Total	16616970	13440533	3176437	74.41	72.16	88.82
All Assam	19507017	15988262	3518755	73.18	70.44	88.88

Source: Census of India 2011.

As per rural literacy as well as urban literacy rates are concerned Bodo inhabited districts lagged behind than the state average and other districts of Assam. However, growth rate in literacy among the concerned districts was significantly lower than the other districts and the state as a whole. Literacy rates among rural and urban in the state are higher than our concerned districts and other districts in the state.

Table 4.11 shows the district wise IMR, CER, EEI and GDI values. The position of Bodo inhabited districts in terms of GDI is different from other districts of the State. District-wise examination shows poor performance and large variation in gender related development index in the State of Assam. The GDI moves from the highest of 0.877 in NC Hills district followed by Morigaon (0.759), Jorhat (0.701), Kamrup (0.642) and Dibrugarh districts (0.642) which are above the State average (0.537) to the lowest of 0.012 in Karimganj District. The area which has covered 18 districts other than Bodo inhabited districts has scored average GDI value of 0.537 whereas Bodo inhabited districts scored GDI value as poor as 0.383 as per Assam human development report (2003). All the districts of Bodo inhabited area score low level of GDI values which remained below the State average.

In terms of children enrolment ratio (CER), Bodo inhabited districts exhibit 52.17 for male and 41.00 for female respectively which are far below as compared to other districts and the state average, again Bodo inhabited districts show less infant mortality rate (IMR) for male and slightly higher for female than the state average as well as other districts of the state. Estimated Earned Income (EEI) both for male and female are below in Bodo inhabited districts than the state average as well as other districts of Assam. From this analysis it is seen that Bodo inhabited districts are lagging behind in various aspects than the state average and other districts of the state.

Table 4.11
Gender related development index, 2001

District	CER (2001)		IMR		EEI		GDI Index	GDI Rank
	Male	Female	Male	Female	Male	Female		
1	2	3	4	5	6	7	8	9
Barpeta	47.36	39.39	97	104	13,595	2,629	0.448	10
Bongaigaon	50.82	42.23	93	124	7,218	2,255	0.376	16
Darrang	46.19	38.32	118	86	6,204	1,840	0.317	18
Kokrajhar	42.02	32.31	56	75	5,779	2,959	0.418	11
Nalbari	60.94	51.33	102	70	6,540	2,103	0.357	17
Sub Total	52.17	41.00	93	92	7867	2357	0.383	14
Cachar	56.91	49.68	99	85	10,387	2,379	0.409	14
Dhemaji	60.20	46.96	113	117	4,690	3,148	0.410	13
Dhubri	41.35	31.27	123	132	7,667	1,269	0.206	21
Goalpara	47.58	39.65	109	103	9,475	2,473	0.413	12

(Contd...)

1	2	3	4	5	6	7	8	9
Golaghat	58.22	50.31	66	56	13,538	5,443	0.608	7
Hailakandi	54.55	43.37	101	97	17,504	4,908	0.609	6
Jorhat	64.62	56.75	47	48	20,208	7,336	0.701	3
Kamrup	64.03	57.48	80	78	20,462	5,347	0.642	4
Lakhimpur	60.83	52.83	138	104	6,173	4,366	0.491	8
Morigaon	48.85	43.8	106	97	31,898	8,240	0.759	2
Nagaon	52.62	47.93	104	89	4,617	916	0.068	22
NC Hills	60.95	54.16	109	100	35,248	14,715	0.877	1
Sibsagar	63.49	56.29	81	68	7,478	3,411	0.468	9
Sonitpur	49.9	40.04	76	77	5,936	2,621	0.397	15
Tinsukia	49.63	39.84	82	63	3,964	1,896	0.300	19
Sub Total	55.8	47.44	94	86	12,764	4,459	0.471	11
State Average	53.81	45.61	95	87	6,744	5,530	0.537	

Source: Census of India 2001.

Table-4.12 depicts infant and child mortality rate across the districts of Assam. In Bodo inhabited districts, both infant mortality and child mortality rates are found higher than the State average and also other districts of Assam. It is also seen that people in different districts in Assam were not equally aware enough to medical access facilities because of this mortality rates are found much higher in our concern area.

Table 4.12
Infant and child mortality rate (2001)

District	*Infant Mortality Rate*		*Child Mortality Rate*	
	Male	*Female*	*Male*	*Female*
Barpeta	97	104	145	139
Bongaigaon	93	124	135	150
Darrang	118	86	131	131
Kokrajhar	56	75	96	114
Nalbari	102	7	113	121
Sub Total	93	91	124	131
Cachar	99	85	122	111
Dhemaji	113	117	140	138
Dhubri	123	132	169	162
Dibrugarh	56	45	76	78
Goalpara	109	103	138	127
Golaghat	66	56	97	91
Jorhat	47	48	78	76
Kamrup	80	78	92	97
K. Anglong	76	75	125	124
Lakhimpur	138	104	120	130
Morigaon	106	97	141	127
NC Hills	109	100	119	116
Sibsagar	81	68	85	92
Sonitpur	75	77	115	101
Tinsukia	82	63	90	80
Sub Total	92	85	116	112
State Average	92	86	118	116

Source: Assam Human Development report, 2003.

Household Amenities

It is important to note that majority of the households that could not build Pucca houses in the state of Assam. As per Assam Human Development Report 2003, about 12.88 per cent households in the state were having their own Pucca houses. In Bodo inhabited districts, it was 9.12 per cent whereas other district had 14.65 per cent. It is also seen that people in different districts in Assam were not equally rich enough to construct Pucca houses. In Bodo inhabited districts, it ranges from 10.15 per cent to 7.89 per cent. The people in Nalbari district were having highest Pucca houses of 10.55 per cent and the lowest was in Baksa district of 7.89 per cent only.

In case of semi-Pucca houses, 12.80 per cent people were having semi-Pucca houses in the state where the corresponding figure was 13.84 per cent in Bodo inhabited districts. People in Bodo area were having more semi-Pucca houses than the state average which has confirmed from the above information. About 65.59 per cent households were having Kutcha houses in Assam. In Bodo inhabited districts it was 77.28 per cent of people were having Kutcha houses which indicates that people in this area were quite poor. It also indicates that people are not enough to build Pucca and semi-Pucca houses.

It has been seen that about 37.43 per cent of the households had toilet facilities within the premises of their residence in Assam, whereas the corresponding figure was 24.12 per cent only in Bodo inhabited districts (Table 4.13). But 41.13 per cent of the households were having toilet facilities in other districts in the state. It was observed that in Bodo inhabited districts less number of households were having this facility than the state average as well as other districts. In this sense as per development criteria our concern area is lagged behind the other districts and the state as a whole.

Table 4.13
Households amenities, 2001

District	*HPH*	*HSPH*	*HKH*	*TF*	*SDW*	*EAH*
Barpeta	7.89	13.21	78.89	39.42	40.45	11.32
Bongaigaon	10.04	15.53	74.53	28.21	20.46	14.10
Darrang	9.52	14.88	75.60	18.62	46.66	12.40
Kokrajhar	9.33	17.17	76.84	14.41	18.93	12.16
Nalbari	10.15	9.47	79.98	17.05	64.69	9.00
Sub-Total	9.12	13.84	77.28	24.12	40.16	11.56
Cachar	3.34	5.06	91.60	63.26	20.07	3.52
Dhemaji	2.26	4.12	93.65	16.37	48.58	11.67
Dhubri	29.4	13.06	57.54	29.64	56.10	26.39
Dibrugarh	8.10	14.23	77.67	48.18	67.32	11.67
Goalpara	12.29	16.19	71.31	37.89	31.83	17.33
Golaghat	10.22	11.82	78.16	32.32	59.50	19.03
Hailakandi	23.63	26.47	49.90	60.97	18.54	25.16
Jorhat	23.22	20.52	56.27	29.82	47.28	33.82
Kamrup	5.64	4.25	89.92	49.76	57.71	12.94
K. Anglong	13.51	12.23	74.27	24.94	33.88	32.84
Karimganj	10.79	14.17	75.04	73.17	17.83	13.83
Lakhimpur	6.81	10.27	82.91	24.88	29.03	11.02
Morigaon	12.39	12.59	75.02	24.55	62.67	17.07
Nagaon	15.3	11.78	72.92	41.77	65.32	22.90
NC Hills	21.83	27.45	50.71	34.61	45.54	26.72
Sibsagar	18.71	10.82	70.47	32.18	54.36	16.32
Sonitpur	30.88	11.74	57.38	29.99	27.50	23.88
Tinsukia	14.48	13.65	71.85	53.65	73.96	19.40
Sub-Total	14.65	11.81	73.44	41.13	47.73	20.56
State Average	12.88	12.80	65.59	37.43	45.86	17.75

Source: Assam Human Development Report 2003.

HPH=Households having Pucca House, HSPH=Households having Semi Pucca House,

HKH=Households having Kutcha House, TF=Toilet Facility, SDW=Safe Drinking Water.

EAH=Electricity At Home.

However, there were significant inter-districts variations in access to toilet facilities in the state of Assam. The Bodo inhabited districts had low access to toilet facilities. Among the districts in Bodo area, it was 39.42 per cent in Barpeta district of which households had access to this facility and the lowest of 14.41 per cent were availed by the households in Kokrajhar district. But in case of other districts other than Bodo area, had more access to this facility. Districts like Karimganj had 73.17 per cent, followed by Cachar district 63.27 per cent, Hailakandi 60.97 per cent, Tinsukia 53.65 per cent, Kamrup 49.76 per cent, Dibrugarh 48.18 per cent, Nagaon district 41.77 per cent and Goalpara district 37.89 per cent, NC Hills 34.61 per cent. All these districts had more access to toilet facilities than the state average (34.57 per cent). The average of other district access to this facility was 41.13 per cent whereas in Bodo inhabited districts it was only 24.12 per cent.

Regarding safe drinking water, as per Human Development Report-2003, as low as 45.86 per cent households in the state was having access to safe drinking water as compared to 40.16 per cent in Bodo inhabited districts (Table 4.11). When 35.07 per cent and 42.56 per cent of households had access to safe drinking water in rural and urban areas respectively in Bodo inhabited districts, the corresponding figures for the state were as high as 43.28 per cent and 64.07 per cent. Thus Bodo inhabited districts have been a laggard in case of access to safe drinking water, further, there was wide spread inter-districts variations both in rural and urban areas. The rural-urban gap has been seen widely in Bodo area than the state average.

Electricity or power is the prime mover of the economic development. The available of cheap, abundant and regular power supply is essential condition for development and also one of the important determinants of the quality of life. There is a direct relationship in the growth of the consumption of the power and that of the economy. The state of Assam possesses vast potential for generation of power or electricity based on its locally available water, natural gas, coal and oil resources. Assam alone has 28 per cent of the total hydropower potential of the country which remains underutilized. Besides, gas is also available in plenty which can also be a good source of power in the state but due to a variety of factors it has not been possible to carry out exploitation of power resources in the state to its fullest. So, Assam lags far behind the national average in the field of power development In Assam while the number of villages that have been electrified has decreased from 82 per cent in 1991 to 72 per cent in 2006, yet we find that as many as 28 per cent of the rural people do not have access to electricity. This is due to the fact that a village is declared as electrified if power reaches the village even the though few of the houses may have connection. Moreover, among the districts of Assam Darrang district had the largest number of electrified villages 1211 in 2006 while it was lowest in the Hailakandi district with only 254 villages. It is important to note that almost of the districts have not achieved noticeable per centage of village electrification; a vast majority of the households do not have access to electricity. Around 17.75 per cent of households in Assam had access to electricity in their home as against the figure of only 11.56 per cent in Bodo inhabited districts, whereas other districts had access to electricity at 20.56 per cent.

Distribution of Academic Institutions

Table 4.14 tells us wide variations of distribution of academic institutions across the districts in Assam. Total number of institutions in Bodo inhabited districts was only 44 as pre-primary schools, 6889 primary schools, 2404 middle schools, 1139 high schools, 135 higher secondary schools and 44 junior colleges. The area had a total population of 6110944 as per 2001. If we analyse their number for per lakh population distribution we visualized the following

Table 4.14
Number of academic institutions 2001

District	*Pre-primary school*	*Primary school*	*Middle School*	*High School*	*Higher Secondary*	*Junior College*
Barpeta	17	1840	693	290	42	10
Bongaigaon	5	966	340	187	19	1
Darrang	11	1523	450	232	31	10
Kokrajhar	2	1076	323	132	15	3
Nalbari	9	1484	598	298	28	20
Sub-Total	44	6889	2404	1139	135	44
Cachar	2	1610	408	218	28	3
Dhemaji	9	847	302	223	15	3
Dhubri	—	1449	607	156	34	4
Dibrugarh	12	1335	322	156	25	2
Goalpara	—	942	302	152	13	1
Golaghat	7	1004	343	164	23	4
Hailakandi	2	1003	323	49	11	-
Jorhat	18	1570	449	253	26	8
Kamrup	49	2182	762	504	72	19
K. Anglong	—	1416	372	197	12	2
Karimganj	4	1245	327	92	25	1
Lakhimpur	1	1378	648	334	25	12
Morigaon	—	816	283	138	14	6
Nagaon	21	2038	651	304	60	3
NC Hills	—	712	214	—		
Sibsagar	12	1713	472	191	41	9
Sonitpur	13	1386	314	238	36	5
Tinsukia	5	964	213	186	19	5
Sub-Total	155	23610	7312	3555	479	87
State Average	199	30499	9716	4776	620	131

Source: Statistical Hand Book- 2001 & 2007, Government of Assam.

observation. In regard to over all distribution of academic institutions, the condition of Bodo inhabited districts is more or less equivalent to other districts in the state of Assam. As against the other district figure of .7545 pre-primary schools for per lakh population, the Bodo inhabited district has only .7200 pre-primary schools per lakh population. Whereas number of primary school was only 112.732 in Bodo inhabited district as against the figure of 114.921 in other district [Table-4.14]. In case of middle school, the figure was 39.3393 for per lakh population in Bodo inhabited district which was slightly more then the corresponding figure 35.5909 in other district. In case of number of high school and higher secondary school, distribution of these institutions was more or less equivalent in Bodo inhabited district and other district as well as the state level. But in regard to Junior Colleges the condition of Bodo inhabited district (figure.7200) was better off as compared to other district (figure.4235) in the state.

Distribution of Health Care Institutions

Table 4.16 shows of distribution of health care institutions in the districts of Assam. Total number of hospitals in Bodo inhabited districts was only six whereas the corresponding figure in the state was twenty four of which eighteen were in other districts.

In case of Public Health Centre facilities, in Bodo inhabited districts its figure was 178, however distribution of it varied across the districts in the state as well as in Bodo inhabited districts. In Bodo inhabited districts it ranges from 9 to 25 numbers. Total number of Public Health Centre was 610 in the state. Distribution of Community Health Centre in the districts of Assam tells further wide variation across the districts. There was only 29 Community Health Centre in Bodo inhabited districts which cover about 61.10 lakhs of population in the area. However, total number of Community

Table 4.15

Number of academic institutions (per lakh population. 2001)

District	*Pre-Primary*	*Primary*	*Middle*	*High School*	*Higher Secondary*	*Junior College*
1	*2*	*3*	*4*	*5*	*6*	*7*
Barpeta	1.0321	111.7046	42.0714	17.6056	2.5498	0.6071
Bongaigaon	0.5526	106.7598	37.5759	20.6667	2.0998	0.1105
Darrang	0.7312	101.2418	29.9138	15.4222	2.0607	0.6647
Kokrajhar	0.2208	118.7947	35.6605	14.5733	1.6561	0.3312
Nalbari	0.7834	129.1756	52.0532	25.9396	2.4373	1.7409
Sub Total	0.7200	112.732	39.3393	18.6387	2.2091	0.7200
Cachar	0.1384	111.4248	28.2368	15.0873	1.9378	0.2076
Dhemaji	1.5736	148.0914	52.8024	38.9898	2.6226	0.5245
Dhubri	0	88.4969	37.0722	9.5276	2.0765	0.2443
Dibrugarh	1.01259	112.6514	27.1713	13.1637	2.1096	0.1688
Goalpara	0	114.5937	36.7381	18.4907	1.5814	0.1216

(Contd...)

1	2	3	4	5	6	7
Golaghat	0.7397	106.0998	35.2472	17.3310	2.4306	0.4227
Hailakandi	0.3684	184.7581	59.4984	9.0261	2.0263	0
Jorhat	1.8014	157.1224	44.935	25.3197	2.6020	0.8006
Kamrup	1.9426	86.50752	30.2102	19.9816	2.8545	0.7533
K. Anglong	0	174.1031	45.7389	24.2219	1.4754	0.2459
Karimganj	0.3968	123.5148	32.4412	9.1272	2.4802	0.0992
Lakhimpur	0.1125	155.0039	72.8901	37.5699	2.8121	1.3498
Morigaon	0	105.12	36.4570	17.7776	1.8035	0.7729
Nagaon	0.9073	88.04867	28.1255	13.1338	2.5922	0.1296
NC Hills	0	378.5643	113.782	0	0	0
Sibsagar	1.1409	162.8736	44.8782	18.1604	3.8983	0.8557
Sonitpur	0.7731	82.4258	18.6737	14.1539	2.1409	0.2973
Tinsukia	0.4347	83.8216	18.5207	16.1730	1.6521	0.4347
Sub Total	0.7545	114.921	35.5909	17.3038	2.3315	0.4235
State	0.7466	114.419	36.4502	17.9175	2.3259	0.4914

Source: Statistical Hand Book- 2001 & 2007, Government of Assam.

Health Centre was only 100 in the state, 71 of it distributed among other districts in the state.

Table 4.16
Distribution of health care institutions (2001)

District	*Hospital*	*P.H.C.*	*Dispen-saries*	*Hospital Beds*	*C.H.C*	*Sub-Centre*
Barpeta	1	41	9	340	6	152
Bongaigaon	1	23	20	156	4	95
Darrang	1	35	11	352	7	322
Kokrajhar	2	37	25	414	3	198
Nalbari	1	42	14	512	9	280
Sub Total	6	178	79	1853	29	1047
Cachar	—	22	18	152	2	288
Dhemaji	1	9	5	208	3	88
Dhubri	1	23	21	422	6	303
Dibrugarh	1	37	4	192	5	180
Goalpara	1	17	22	260	1	192
Golaghat	1	32	14	410	5	212
Hailakandi	1	8	3	154	1	103
Jorhat	1	24	10	472	4	149
Kamrup	2	51	50	648	9	338
K. Anglong	1	35	13	454	5	159
Lakhimpur	1	23	5	292	5	187
Morigaon	1	13	19	178	2	111
Nagaon	1	38	22	524	9	464
NC Hills	1	12	2	178	2	73
Sibsagar	1	30	10	308	2	227
Sonitpur	2	28	20	504	5	325
Tinsukia	1	14	5	244	4	236
SubTotal	18	432	252	5681	71	4062
State Average	24	610	331	7534	100	5109

Source: Statistical Hand Book- 2001& 2007, Govt. of Assam.
Note: P.H.C=Public Health Centre, C.H.C=Community Health Centre.

In other words, Bodo inhabited district figure of hospital was .0982 for per lakh population as against the figure of .0876 in other district of the state. In regard to heath care services, the condition of Bodo inhabited district was better off as compared to other district in the state. As against the Bodo inhabited figure of 30.3226 hospital beds for per lakh population, other district has only 27.6521 hospital beds per lakh population. In regard to public health centre and dispensary, the condition is over all equivalents in both Bodo inhabited district ant other district in the state. In case of sub-centre services, the number was only 17.1332 for per lakh population in Bodo inhabited district whereas the corresponding figure was 19.7716 per lakh population in other district in the state [Table-4.17]. Relating to the Community Health Centre services, the condition was slightly (figure .4745) better off in Bodo inhabited district as compared to other district (figure.3456) in the state of Assam. The overall situation shows that relatively Bodo inhabited districts were more developed as compared to other districts in the state of Assam. However, though there is more numbers of such facilities in our concern area its distribution are more concentrated in few places only whereas certain areas lack from such facilities. In other words, its distribution are highly scattered with no reasonable distribution across the districts in the concern area. In the case of hospital bed facilities distribution more disparity is found across the districts in our concern area. But in the case of installation of public health centers more or less same scattered were found among the concern districts. But if we analyses installations of such facilities across the districts in the state of Assam, in general more or less equitable distribution found but actually few places absorbed more installation of certain such facilities resulting wide disparity across the districts.

Urbanization

Urbanization is a phenomenon, which is part and parcel of economic development in general. Urbanization, thus, refers to the process of population concentration entailing on

Table 4.17

Distribution of health care institutions (per lakh population, 2001)

District	*Hospital*	*PHC*	*Dispensary*	*Hospital Beds*	*C.H.C.*	*Sub Centre*
1	*2*	*3*	*4*	*5*	*6*	*7*
Barpeta	0.0607	2.4891	0.5464	20.6411	0.3642	9.2278
Bongaigaon	0.1105	2.5419	2.2103	17.2407	0.4421	10.4991
Darrang	0.0665	2.3266	0.7312	23.3993	0.4653	21.4050
Kokrajhar	0.2208	4.0850	2.7601	45.7073	0.3312	21.8599
Nalbari	0.0870	3.6559	1.2186	44.5673	0.7834	24.3727
Sub Total	0.0982	2.9128	1.2928	30.3226	0.4745	17.1332
Cachar	0	1.5226	1.2457	10.5196	0.1384	19.9319
Dhemaji	0.1748	1.5736	0.8742	36.3672	0.5245	15.3861
Dhubri	0.0611	1.4047	1.2826	25.7734	0.3664	18.5056
Dibrugarh	0.0844	3.1222	0.3375	16.2015	0.4219	15.1889
Goalpara	0.1216	2.0680	2.6763	31.6288	0.1216	23.3567
Golaghat	0.1057	3.3817	1.4795	43.3276	0.5284	22.4035

(Contd...)

1	2	3	4	5	6	7
Hailakandi	0.1842	1.4736	0.5526	28.3676	0.1842	18.9732
Jorhat	0.1001	2.4019	1.0008	47.2368	0.4003	14.9116
Kamrup	0.0793	2.0219	1.9823	25.6906	0.3568	13.4003
K. Anglong	0.1229	4.3034	1.5984	55.8212	0.6148	19.5497
Karimganj	0.0992	1.5873	0.8929	15.8734	0.0992	23.0164
Lakhimpur	0.1125	2.5871	0.5624	32.8455	0.5624	21.0346
Morigaon	0.1288	1.6747	2.4476	22.9306	0.2576	14.2994
Nagaon	0.0432	1.6417	0.9505	22.6386	0.3888	20.0464
NC Hills	0.5317	6.3803	1.0634	94.6411	1.0634	38.8135
Sibsagar	0.0951	2.8524	0.9508	29.2849	0.1902	21.5834
Sonitpur	0.1189	1.6651	1.1894	29.9730	0.2973	19.3278
Tinsukia	0.0869	1.2173	0.4347	21.2162	0.3478	20.5206
Sub Total	0.0876	2.1027	1.2266	27.6521	0.3456	19.7716
State Average	0.0900	2.2883	1.21418	28.2643	0.3751	19.1667

Source: Statistical Hand Book- 2001& 2007, Govt. of Assam.
Note: P.H.C=Public Health Centre, C.H.C=Community Health Centre.

increase in population living in urban areas. It has been considered not only as an index of economic development but also as an important factor of social change. Urbanization is not a mechanized process but it is governed by economic, social and cultural factors and the process of rural to urban migration is by far the vital components. As Tadaro remarked that migration is accelerated mainly by rational economic consideration of relative belief and the decision to migrate depends on expected economic difference. The provision of urban services such as transport, communication, water, sanitation and shelter alone is usually unlikely to stimulate large-scale urban development. Thus planning of urban development should essentially be supportive of economic development in the state of underprivileged area in the tertiary sector.

Table 4.18 shows that in 1991, 5.82 per cent people were residing in urban area in Bodo inhabited districts which was increased to 6.59 per cent in 2001. Urban population varies from district to district in the state. In Bodo inhabited districts it ranges from 2.31 per cent to 9.14 per cent in 1991. Where 9.14 per cent was in Bongaigaon district which was the highest and lowest was 2.31 per cent in Nalbari district in Bodo inhabited districts, whereas other districts shows a wide variation across the districts from 1.86 per cent to 32.76 per cent in the same year. However, Kamrup district had highest per centage of urban population of (32.76 per cent) and lowest was of (1.86 per cent) in Dhemaji district in 1991. Urban population in the other districts was 12.74 per cent which was increased to 14.78 per cent in 2001. However, per centage of urban population in other districts was more than the state average both in 1991 and 2001. In case of Bodo inhabited districts, urbanization is still quite low as compared to both other districts and State average.

Bodo inhabited districts as one of the areas is not only at a low level of urbanization, but it is characterized by regional

1	2	3	4	5		
Barpeta	1288341	97318	1520333	126868	7.02	7.62
Bongaigaon	733669	73854	795053	109782	9.14	12.17
Darrang	1234876	63984	1429492	74828	4.93	4.91
Kokrajhar	749935	50724	841823	63941	6.33	6.84
Nalbari	992915	23475	1121338	27486	2.31	2.41
Sub Total	4999736	309355	5708839	402905	5.82	6.59
Cachar	1096161	119224	1243534	201387	9.81	13.97
Dhemaji	469939	8891	533112	38832	1.86	6.91
Dhubri	1170494	161981	1444901	192443	12.15	11.66
Dibrugarh	858877	183580	956634	228438	17.61	18.77
Goalpara	616042	52096	755133	66902	7.80	8.18

(Contd...)

1	2	3	4	5	6	7
Golaghat	779258	48838	865141	81138	5.90	8.37
Hailakandi	414910	34138	498787	44085	7.60	8.39
Jorhat	738174	133032	827901	171320	15.27	16.91
Kamrup	1344856	655215	1614107	908217	32.76	35.81
K. Anglong	592257	70466	721381	91930	10.63	11.42
Lakhimpur	202387	49130	823857	65153	6.54	7.32
Morigaon	606693	32989	738268	37988	5.16	4.91
Nagaon	1687449	205722	2036342	278287	10.87	12.00
NC Hills	116315	34486	128644	59435	22.87	31.19
Sibsagar	842294	65689	954557	97179	7.23	9.22
Sonitpur	1320379	103908	1505719	175794	7.29	8.81
Tinsukia	803624	158674	926105	223957	16.49	19.49
SubTotal	13736791	2178440	17508249	3036335	12.74	14.78
State	19926527	2487785	23216288	3439240	11.10	12.72

disparity in the distribution of the urban population. The rate of urban population and urbanization has never been taken place rapid in the area since decades to decades. Economic development is generally accompanied by the relative decline in the role of primary and the rise in the role of secondary and tertiary sectors of the economy. Urbanization implies economic development. But Bodo inhabited districts being basically an agricultural area of the state has undue structure is not conducive and stands in the way of rural industrialization of the state which is mainly due to acute communication, transport and other infrastructural facilities and has kept the area in isolation and thus deprived its due share in acquiring the knowledge of modernization.

Distribution of Workers

Working force in a society refers to that portion of population, which is engaged in various productive activities in an economy. It refers to the number of people who are actually working and contributing to the national income. The economic progress depends upon the size of the working force. Larger the number of working force more shall be the production in the state leading to higher income and better level of living for the people.

The size of labour force in an economy depends upon various factors such as the age composition, life expectancy and availability of work, etc. The size of labour force is an important factor, which affects the entire stream of production, savings and capital formation. A smaller proportion of labour force in the total population would imply a relatively larger proportion of dependency and vice versa. Occupational structure of a society is closely interlinked with its economic development. In the advanced countries a very large proportion of working force is engaged in tertiary and secondary sector and only a small proportion of workers are engaged in the primary sector. In underdeveloped countries, on the other hand, the largest proportion of workers is engaged in agriculture, while a very small fraction of the working force engaged in secondary and tertiary sectors. Colin Clark writes a high average level of real income per head is always associated with a high proportion of the working population engaged in tertiary industries; low real income per head is always associated with a low proportion of the working population engaged in tertiary production and a high per centage in primary production. A.G.B. Fisher also reaches the same conclusion we may say that in every progressive economy there has been a steady shift of employment and investment from the essential primary activities to secondary activities of all kinds and to still greater extent into tertiary production.

Occupational structure in an underdeveloped country reflects different character, which shows excessive dependence on agriculture. Between secondary and tertiary sectors, a large proportion is engaged in the service sector and a smaller proportion in the industrial sector. In underdeveloped area, because of low incomes, large part of income gets used up in purchasing food and other agricultural products. Consequently, there is not much demand for goods and services of the industrial and service sector. Further modern capital goods and techniques needed by industries and services are very inadequate in the society for which these sectors are unable to expand and cannot provide large work opportunities for the labour force.

Table-4.19 shows district-wise per centage people engaged in various sectors of the economy in 2001. The total population can be divided into workers and non workers. The workers are those who participate in the economic activities and non workers constitute the dependent population of the society. Greater is the number of non workers population higher is the dependency ratio. The total workers can again be sub-divided into main workers and marginal workers. The total number of main workers in the state of Assam for male was 40.87 per cent and female was 10.39 per cent whereas the same was 42.45 per cent for male and 8.08 per cent for female in our concern area in 2001.

Table 4.19
Distribution of workers

	% of main workers (2001)		*% of workers (2001)*		*% of non-workers (2001)*	
District	*Male*	*Female*	*Male*	*Female*	*Male*	*Female*
Barpeta	42.91	5.70	47.81	14.01	52.19	85.99
Bongaigaon	43.35	7.08	48.74	15.25	5126	84.77
Darrang	44.76	8.14	50.39	20.76	49.61	9.24
Kokrajhar	39.78	11.48	48.37	25.27	51.83	74.73
Nalbari	41.44	8.00	48.34	18.07	51.66	81.93
Sub Total	42.45	8.08	48.73	18.67	51.31	67.33
Cachar	41.85	7.52	49.76	13.67	50.24	86.43
Dhemaji	38.27	15.87	50.09	38.20	49.89	61.80
Dhubri	43.67	4.14	48.55	8.04	51.45	91.96
Goalpara	42.44	7.54	48.41	17.55	51.59	82.45
Golaghat	42.10	14.02	51.49	30.90	48.51	69.10
Hailakandi	41.55	8.10	48.99	16.55	51.01	83.45
Jorhat	42.13	13.39	52.63	29.39	47.37	70.61
K. Anglong	40.88	14.53	49.02	31.42	50.98	68.58
Karimganj	40.40	5.30	47.92	11.85	52.02	88.15
Lakhimpur	45.10	18.97	62.08	49.89	37.92	50.11
Morigaon	14.57	5.81	50.56	16.33	49.44	83.67
Nagaon	42.15	5.31	49.38	12.24	50.62	87.76
NC Hills	43.50	13.20	49.12	24.41	50.88	75.59
Sibsagar	40.02	13.52	51.29	29.62	48.71	70.38
Sonitpur	42.49	11.78	50.17	24.34	49.83	75.66
Tinsukia	42.06	17.85	50.65	29.91	49.35	70.09
SubTotal	40.43	11.03	50.51	23.80	49.48	76.55
State Average	40.87	10.39	50.12	22.68	49.87	74.27

Source: Census Report 2001, Govt. of India.

Total male workers in our concern area are slightly more than the state average as revealed from the table 4.19. As for 2001 census, the per centage of non workers in Bodo inhabited district were 67.33 per cent with the corresponding figure 76.27 per cent in the state. The total male workers in the state constituted 40.12 per cent while the same was 48.73 per cent in Bodo inhabited districts. So, male dependency ratio is higher in our concern area than the state average whereas female dependency ratio is higher in the state as a whole than the concern area.

Table 4.20 reveals district wise work force participation rate in Assam in 2001 per thousand populations. In this case also the work participation rate in Bodo inhabited districts is lesser than the state corresponding figure of 395. In rural areas the work participation rate in Bodo inhabited districts is 485 whereas the whole state figure is 498. However, case study in the rural areas shows that female work participation rate in the concerned five districts is pitiably lesser than the state corresponding figure of 223.

Table 4.21 again attempts to find out distribution of main workers across the districts in Assam. In 1991 total main workers in Bodo inhabited districts was about 3.08 lakh which was increased to 3.14 lakh whereas the same was only 2.79 lakh in other districts of the state in 1991 which was slightly increased to 2.82 lakh in 2001.

In the case of marginal workers other districts of the state is ahead of our concerned area whereas number of non working population was found more in the Bodo inhabited districts than other districts in the state.

Table 4.20
Work participation rate, Assam 2001
(per 1000 population)

	Total			*Rural*		
District	*Person*	*Male*	*Female*	*Person*	*Male*	*Female*
Barpeta	314	478	140	315	476	144
Bongaigaon	325	487	152	327	483	162
Darrang	360	504	208	362	502	214
Kokrajhar	371	484	253	375	480	264
Nalbari	337	483	181	338	483	183
Sub Total	341	487	167	343	485	193
Cachar	322	498	136	323	494	142
Dhemaji	443	501	382	453	501	402
Dhubri	289	486	80	288	485	81
Goalpara	333	484	175	336	483	183
Golaghat	416	515	309	423	513	327
Hailakandi	333	490	165	337	490	172
Jorhat	416	526	294	431	524	329
Kamrup	326	486	148	328	486	158
K. Anglong	406	490	314	417	492	336
Karimganj	304	479	119	303	477	120
Lakhimpur	561	621	499	577	626	525
Morigaon	339	506	153	340	504	187
Nagaon	314	494	122	316	491	129
NC Hills	375	491	244	400	495	294
Sibsagar	409	513	296	414	507	315
Sonitpur	376	502	243	381	499	257
SubTotal	376	503	237	384	504	258
State Average	359	490	208	364	498	223

Source: Census Report 2001, Govt. of India.

Table 4.21

Distribution of workers (in Lakh)

District	*Total main workers*		*Total marginal workers*		*Total non-workers*	
	1991	*2001*	*1991*	*2001*	*1991*	*2001*
Barpeta	3.66	4.08	0.49	1.08	9.69	11.30
Bongaigaon	2.40	2.33	0.30	0.60	5.24	6.11
Darrang	4.05	4.04	0.37	1.23	7.76	9.76
Kokrajhar	2.62	2.34	0.19	1.00	5.14	5.70
Nalbari	2.69	2.91	0.71	0.92	6.79	7.64
Sub Total	3.08	3.14	0.41	0.97	6.92	8.10
Cachar	3.54	3.64	0.26	1.00	8.28	9.79
Dhemaji	1.60	1.55	0.54	0.94	2.63	3.21
Dhubri	3.61	3.99	0.30	0.71	9.40	11.66
Goalpara	2.03	2.09	0.78	0.64	3.83	5.48
Golaghat	2.86	2.69	0.46	1.18	4.88	5.57
Hailakandi	1.29	1.38	0.10	0.41	3.07	3.62
Jorhat	2.99	2.85	0.34	1.29	5.37	5.84
K. Anglong	2.51	2.31	0.31	0.98	3.79	4.82
Karimganj	2.21	2.35	0.16	0.68	5.88	7.04
Lakhimpur	2.41	2.88	0.80	2.09	4.29	3.91
Morigaon	1.84	2.00	0.50	0.62	4.16	5.13
Nagaon	5.53	5.66	1.17	1.61	12.21	15.86
NC Hills	.57	.55	0.05	0.15	.87	1.17
Sibsagar	3.31	2.87	0.49	1.43	5.27	6.21
Sonitpur	4.76	4.65	0.70	1.69	8.51	10.46
Tinsukia	3.51	3.49	0.40	1.16	5.70	6.83
SubTotal	2.79	2.82	0.47	1.35	5.53	6.67
State Total	66.92	71.14	10.96	24.24	143.25	171.16

Source: Census Report 2011, Govt. of India.

Status of Human Development

Concept and Operationalisation

The concept of human development has evolved out as a broader measure of socio-economic progress of a nation/state/ district/block. The first Human Development Report, launched by UNDP in 1990, defined human development as a process of enlarging people's choices. These choices cover social, political, psychological and other aspects of human life. However, for the sake of simplicity only three essential choices viz., to lead a healthy and long life, to acquire knowledge and to have access to the resources needed for a decent standard of living are incorporated in Human Development Index (HDI). Human development is measured in the form of a composite index called as HDI. This composite index includes three dimensions: life expectancy, real GDP per-capita and educational attainment (adult literacy and a combination of primary, secondary and tertiary) reflecting the human achievement. The composite index (HDI) intends to capture three most critical dimensions of human well-being: health, education and income. According to the latest formulation of UNDP (HDR, 1999) three dimensions are computed with the help of four indicators: life expectancy to capture the health attainment, adult literacy rate and combined enrolment ratio for the educational attainment and real GDP per capita (in PPP US $) for the command over resources. The other important choices of human life such as Human rights, political participation etc are not incorporated because of the complexity involved in it. For this the HDI is often described as the poor index representing the vast concept of human Development. However, there are studies across the globe which attempt to add the other area of these aspects of human life into the measurement of human development. Hence, Human Development Index quantifies a country's typical achievement in three main dimensions of human life.

Although, HDI was widely extolled as a major policy instrument and a useful policy tool a few year after its emergence, it was recognized first as a measure of average achievements in human development. It neither reflected the deprivation nor the distributional aspects of development, particularly the issue of inequality.

Human development is assumed to have two sides. One is the formation of human capabilities such as improved health, knowledge and skill. The other side is the people make use of their acquired capabilities for productive purposes, social and political affairs as well as ensure equitable access to human opportunities. If the scales of human development do not fairly balance the two sides then considerable human frustration may result. In this sense income is clearly one of the options that people would like to have resulting failure to give the sum total of lives. Human development is of the people, for the people and by the people. Of the people refers to human capital formation a... human resources development through nutrition, health and education. For the people stressing the need for the benefits of economic growth to be translated into peoples' lives and by the people meaning that people must be able to influence a process that affects their lives (Jahan, 2005).

The current focus on human development has, however, served to highlight the gender dimension and continuing inequalities confronting women. In 1995, the Human Development Report introduced the concept of Gender related Development Index (GDI) including other indices such as Gender Empowerment Measure (GEM). While GDI measures the achievements in the same dimensions and variables as the HDI, it also takes into account inequality in achievement between women and men (Anand and Sen, 1995). The greater the gender disparity in human development, the lower is country's GDI compared to its HDI. The GDI is the HDI adjusted downwards for gender inequality. On the other hand, GEM indicates whether women are able to actively participate in economic and political life. It focuses on participation, measuring gender inequality in key areas of economic and political participation and decision-making. It thus differs from the GDI, an indicator of gender inequality in basic capabilities. The exercises with the GDI and GEM have established that greater gender equality in building human capabilities or providing opportunities to women does not depend on income level or stage of development. And it can be achieved across a range of cultures. As is well known, the women being the less privileged class needs special attention for their development. Contrary to the general belief that development is gender neutral, statistics show that women lag behind men all over the world in almost every aspects of life. It is for this reason that Human Development Report (1995) gives special emphasis on this issue and notes that without empowering women overall development of human beings is not possible. It further stresses that if development is not engendered, is endangered.

Recently the concept of human poverty index (HPI) was introduced in 1997 and it is a composite index measuring the lack of basic human development similar to the three dimensions of the HDI (UNDP 1997). HPI, therefore, focuses on deprivation in the three essential aspects of human life as reflected in the HDI. The third aspect is represented by a multiple of three variables- the percentage of people with access to safe water and health services, and per centage of less than five years old being malnourished. However, human development is the combination of people's entitlement and attainment relating to education, health and livelihood. These three areas, taken together form the everyday experience of development for the people as individuals and as members of a community, state or nation. The concept of human development is a people-centred approach to development where the primary concern is enhancement of human well-being. Human development therefore corresponds to a holistic approach in the process of development.

Summing up it may be noted that the concept of human development is much broader and more complex than any summary measure can captures. The HDI is not a comprehensive measure. It is does not include important aspects of human development, notably the ability to participate in the decisions that affect one's life and to enjoy the respect of others in the community. The indices gives an overview of some basic dimensions of human development, by the must be complemented by looking at the underlying data and other indicators.

Measurement of Human Development

The HDI is a composite index of three basic components of human development, viz., longevity, knowledge and standard of living. Longevity is measured by life expectancy. Knowledge is measured by a combination of adult literacy having two-third weight and mean years of schooling with one-third weight. Standard of living is measured by purchasing power, based on real GDP per capita adjusted for the local cost of living (purchasing power parity, or ppp). The breakthrough for the HDI, however, was to find a common measuring rod for the socio-economic distance traveled. The HDI sets a minimum and a maximum for each dimension and then shows where each country stands in relation to these scales.

It is expressed in terms of a numerical value between 0 and 1. Income above the average world income is adjusted using a progressively higher discount rate. The scores for the three dimensions are then averaged in an overall index.

As we know HDI is a composite index of three basic components of human development such as longevity, knowledge and standard of living. The index is constructed by using the following formula:

$$(1)\ldots\ldots\ldots\ldots HDI_j = \frac{1}{3}(I_1 + I_2 + I_3)$$

Where I_1 (Education Index) and I_2 (Health Index) are constructed by using the formula:

$$(2)\ldots\ldots\ldots\ldots I_j = \frac{X_{ij} - Min(X)}{Max(X_i) - Min(X_i)}$$

And the I_3 (Income Index) is constructed by using the formula:

$$(3)\ldots\ldots\ldots\ldots I_3 = \frac{Log(X_{ij}) - Log\{Min(X_i)\}}{Log\{Max(X_i)\} - Log\{Min(X_i)\}}$$

Thus, while HDI reveals the average achievement in life, GDI adjusts the average achievement to reflect the inequality between men and women in the same dimension as HDI.

Human Development in Assam

There are several attempts to measure the human development in Assam. NCAER (2004) focuses on poor parameters. According to this report, Assam is distinctly a laggard in terms of important indicators of socio-economic well being even among the states of north east India. Although in case of effective literacy, the state Assam is ahead of the national average, the gender disparity in literacy rate in Assam is as high as 15.9 per cent. The rural-urban disparity in respect of literacy is also quite pronounced in Assam. Among the north-east states the drop out rate is also higher in Assam. Assam's position in respect of life expectancy at birth is worse than that of India for both males and females. Expectation of life at birth of males and females is 58.7 years and 58.5 years respectively, whereas for the country as a whole was 60.6 years for males and 61.7 years for females respectively. This is worse than that of India for both males and females. Men live longer than women in Assam though for the country as a whole, women live longer than men. In regard to health care services, the condition of Assam is worse off as compared to other north-east states. As against the all India figure of 0.73 hospital beds for every thousand population, Assam has only 0.06 hospital beds per thousand populations.

According to NHDR (2001), Assam scores HDI values as poor as 0.272 in 1981 and 0.348 in 1991 as against the national averages of 0.302 and 0.381 respectively. The relative position of the state in terms of HDI is also disappointing. In both the years Assam ranks 26 in the field of 28 States and 7 Union Territories. For the year 2001, HDI were constructed only for 15 major states where Assam scored HDI equivalent to 0.386 and placed in the rank of second worst state in the country. It then appears that Assam's shortfall in HDI relatively to national average had reduced during 1980s; however, increased during 1990s. More precisely in 1981 the HDI shortfall is estimated as 11 per cent which reduced to 9.5 per cent in 1991 while increased steadily to 22.3 per cent in 2001.In terms of educational index, the rank of Assam is six with educational attainment index value of 0.4187 (Gol, 1996). The per capita real state domestic product index of Assam is 0.28 and its rank is eight out of fifteen major states (Gol, 1995). As per urbanization index, the rank of Assam is in the last in the fifteen major states, with urbanization index value of 0.11(CMIE, 1996).

In the case of socio-economic development of north east India, Assam rank stood 2nd 77.7 per cent points in the fray where Mizoram stands first with 82 per cent. This index has been measured after giving due weightage to infrastructure available in the respective state for agriculture, banking, electricity, transport, communication, education, health and civil administration. Assam attained literacy rate 63.25

occupying 11th position among the states of India and among the north eastern states; its position was 6th in 2001. Women literacy rate in Assam recorded 54.61per cent in 2001 against 34.29 per cent in 1991. The economy of the state is therefore encouraging and in better position than before. The sectoral contribution of the state's economy has undergone some changes over the years. During the 10th plan period, between 2002-03 and 2006-07 the share of primary sector has declined from 38.89 per cent to 36.55 per cent and the share of secondary sector has increased from 14.23 per cent to 16.62 per cent. As regard the poverty eradication Assam recorded least number of families living below the poverty line with further declining trend as is evident from the figure of 36.09 per cent in 1999-2000 to 19.7 per cent in 2004-05 as against the corresponding figure of 27.50 per cent and 26.10 per cent respectively at the national level.

Life expectancy at birth (LEB) in Assam is below that of the country as a whole, and is one of the lowest amongst major Indian States. There is a very significant gap between the LEB for rural and for urban areas. In the period 1992-96, the LEB in urban areas was 64.6 years. In rural areas it was almost ten years less, at 55.6 years. The per centage of people who are not expected to live beyond 40 years in Assam was also higher than the national average. It was 24.9 per cent in 1981 and 21.8 per cent in 1991. Life Expectancy at Birth (LEB) for women has improved significantly in Assam in recent decades, but continues to be below the average for the country. Women in Assam can expect to live 5.2 years less than their counterparts in the rest of the country. Both men and women in rural Assam can however expect to live almost 10 years less than their urban counterparts.

The IMR is one of the most important indicators of the health status because of its correlation with a number of health and economics characteristic like poverty, illiteracy health and education of the mother, access to health care facilities and so on. In 1990s there was a secular decline in the Infant Mortality Rate in Assam, from 81 per 1000 live births in 1991 to 76 per 1000 live births by the end of the decade, 1999. This is a positive development, but the IMR in Assam is higher than the national average. The Crude Birth Rate (CBR) has declined significantly in Assam, over the last few decades, but it continues to be higher than the national average. The Total Fertility Rate (TFR) was 3.3 children per woman in 1995-97, a substantial decline from 1980-81, when it was as high as 4.1 children. The TFR for all India was 3.4 during the period 1995-97. There is a substantial rural-urban gap in fertility rates as well. The Crude Death Rate (CDR) is another indicator of the health status of a population. The death rate in Assam declined quite substantially in the early nineties, but in the mid nineties, the decline came to a virtual standstill and the rate even showed a marginal increase. As in the case of the CBR, the CDR in rural Assam is substantially higher than that in urban Assam, and the same is true for rural and urban north eastern states of India.

At present, Assam has total road length of approximately 69,000 kms covering both metalled and non-metalled surfaces. That accounts for approximately 60% of the total road length in the North-eastern states of India. In 1998-99 the road length was 33343 km, 8822 km surfaced and 24521 km un-surfaced roads which have shown a great improvement. Upto 30-06-2007, Assam has around 594 telephone exchanges with approximately 11.78 lakh telephone connections of which the number of PCO were 21687, 460344 Landline connections, 84340 WLL subscribers, 600377 mobile users, broadband and internet users in the state. The pattern of consumption of electricity reveals that the consumption was always higher in respect of domestic sector followed by industrial sector and commercial sector of the state. During the year 2006-07 domestic sector accounted for 39.0 per cent of the total consumption of electricity in the state followed by industrial sector 17.0 per cent and commercial sector 12.0 per cent of the total electricity consumption. In the case of infrastructure development Assam is well advance in many aspects than other north eastern states.

According to Ray (2009) there is also poor performance of the state in various aspect of human well-being. Ray elaborates various indicators of Human Development and examined poor performance of human Development in the State of Assam. According to Assam Human Development Report (2003), the state in comparison to the other North Eastern States, ranks below Manipur, Meghalaya, Arunachal Pradesh, Mizoram and Nagaland. The state has not witnessed even slight improvement in some human development indicators in recent decade so the state has long way to go in respect of basic services to the improve health, education and economy, when the judged by the parameters of the Human Development Index and other socio-economic indicators.

The position of Bodo inhabited districts in terms of HDI is different from other districts of the State. District-wise close examination shows poor performance and large variation in human development level in the State of Assam. The HDI moves from the highest of 0.650 in Jorhat district followed by Kamrup (0.574), Golaghat (0.540), Karbi-Anglong (0.494), Morigaon (0.494), Sibsagarh (0.469) and Dibrugarh (0.469) which are above the State average (0.407) to the lowest of 0.214 in Dhubri district. The area which has covered 18 districts other than Bodo inhabited districts has scored average HDI value of 0.408 whereas Bodo inhabited districts scored HDI value as poor as 0.323 as per Assam Human Development Report (2003). All the districts of Bodo inhabited area score low level of HDI values which remained below the State average.

Table 4.22
Human development indicators

District	*Income Index*	*Education Index*	*Health Index*	*HDI Value*	*Rank in HDI*
Barpeta	.385	.527	.473	.396	9
Bongaigaon	.103	.557	.398	.263	21
Darrang	.057	.514	.437	.259	22
Kokrajhar	.145	.474	.555	.354	15
Nalbari	.076	.641	.490	.343	16
Sub Average	.169	.542	.468	.326	
Cachar	.266	.634	.487	.402	8
Dhemaji	.026	.622	.426	.277	20
Dhubri	.102	.454	.376	.214	23
Dibrugarh	.162	.654	.651	.469	6
Goalpara	.146	.536	.455	.308	18
Golaghat	.409	.650	.615	.540	3
Hailakandi	.234	.563	.480	.363	11
Jorhat	.564	.722	.665	.650	1
Kamrup	.573	.701	.558	.574	2
K. Anglong	.491	.535	.562	.494	4
Karimganj	.078	.620	.437	.301	19
Lakhimpur	.154	.657	.433	.337	17
Morigaon	.562	.551	.519	.494	4
Nagaon	.179	.583	.487	.356	14
NC Hills	.211	.650	.448	.363	11
Sibsagar	.242	.702	.565	.469	7
Sonitpur	.071	.552	.558	.357	13
Tinsukia	.082	.571	.573	.377	10
Sub Average	261	.608	.521	.414	
State Average	.286	.595	.506	0.407	

Source: Assam Human Development Report 2003

As earlier mentioned the focused area refers to five districts viz. Barpeta, Bongaigaon, Darrang, Kokrajhar and Nalbari in the State of Assam in which Bodos are largely concentrated. It has been observed that the HDI value moves from the highest of 0.396 in Barpeta district to the lowest of 0.259 in Darrang district which was the second worst district of the state. The average value of HDI in Bodo inhabited districts was 0.323 whereas other districts which are other than Bodo inhabited area districts shows 0.408 which was higher as against the state average of .407.

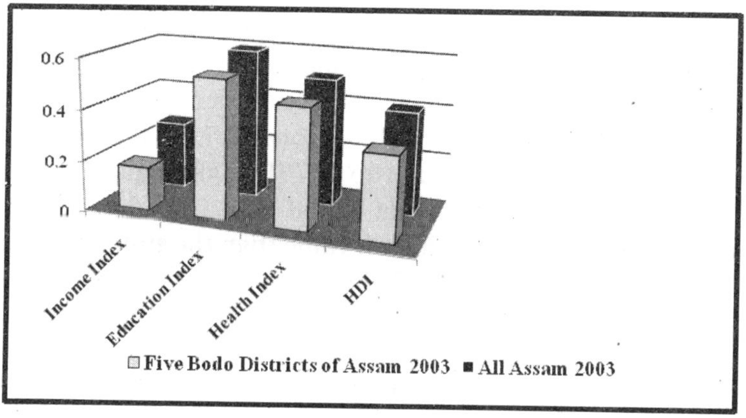

Figure 4.1. Human Development Index: A Comparison

The level of human development across the districts of the Bodo inhabited districts tells a story of deprivation. The HDI ranges from the highest of 0.396 in Barpeta district to the lowest of 0.259 in Darrang district. A low HD level has been observed among the districts of the Bodo area. All districts of the Bodo inhabited area remained below the state average of HDI. Rank 9th in terms of HDI was the highest among five Bodo inhabited districts of the state, where its HDI value is estimated for the district of Barpeta (0.396) which is even lower than the state average of 0.407. The other districts rank within 15 to 22 in the list of 23 districts. In other words, the districts of Barpeta, Kokrajhar, Nalbari, Bongaigaon and Darrang could score HDI of 97.06 per cent, 86.77 per cent, 84.05 per cent, 64.46 per cent and 63.48 per cent respectively of the state average. Other components of HDI such as income, educational and health indices have exhibited a high degree of variation across the state. Further probe into the individual indices provide some interesting findings. Ironically, no districts in the Bodo inhabited area recorded high development in any of the three dimensions. The education index, for these districts varied between a low of 0.474 in Kokrajhar and a high of 0.641 in Nalbari. Nalbari district has the highest education index (0.641) among the districts in Bodo inhabited area and other four districts have low education index than the state average of (0.595). Whereas districts like Jorhat score (0.722) followed by Sibsagar (0.702), then Kamrup (0.701), Lakhimpur (0.657), Dibrugarh (0.654), NC Hills (0.650) and Golaghat (0.650) etc. These districts have higher value than the state average. In case of health index, Bodo inhabited districts had indices ranging within 0.437 and 0.555. All districts in Bodo inhabited area remain below the state average of (0.506) in case of health index except Kokrajhar district (0.555). But districts like Jorhat scored (0.665) followed by Dibrugarh (0.651) in case of health index. In income dimension, the scenario was worsening in various districts of the Bodo inhabited area. Income index lies between the lowest 0.076 to the highest 0.385 in Bodo inhabited districts. Barpeta which is one of the districts of Bodo inhabited area has the highest income dimension of 0.385 which is higher than the state average of 0.286 and other four districts remain below the state average. But districts like Kamrup had 0.573, then followed by Jorhat 0.564 in income dimension which are higher than the state average. Therefore, a high degree of variation in HDI values as well as in the components of the HDI was found across the districts of Assam. The simple coefficient of variation which is often taken as the measures of variation over the cross sectional limits of an economy has been estimated to be as high as 27.99 per cent for overall HDI scores. The corresponding coefficients for these different dimensions of HD (i.e., income, educational and health indices) are 76.15 per cent, 11.74 per cent and 15.07 per cent respectively. Therefore, the variation in income dimension has been maximum while for education dimension the coefficient is minimum.

All districts of the focused area remained below the state average in terms of HDI. The relative position of the districts in focused area is disappointing. It was noticed that Barpeta district scored the highest rank in terms of HDI (rank-9) followed by Kokrajhar (rank-15), Nalbari (rank-16). Whereas other districts as Bongaigaon and Darrang districts took the positions of 21 and 22 respectively in HDI out of the 23 districts in the state of Assam. It is seen that the focused area remained backward in terms of HDI in comparison to other areas of the State and there is a way long to go to bridge the gap.

Conclusion

This Chapter examines the stock of secondary information to evaluate the status of Bodo inhabited districts in terms of human development indicators. Despite the fact that Assam is a poor performer in the country and the districts of our concern are lagging significantly behind in some aspects of development as compared to the state average. However, this observation is not strong enough to draw any inference such that the poor performance in human development triggered the on-going movement for the protection of ethnic identity and thereby overall development.

5

Understanding HRD Among Bodos

Introduction

The objective of human development is not only to produce more goods and services with highest possible efficiency, and to live a luxurious life, but to enhance capabilities of all people to lead full, productive and satisfying lives. The new development paradigm intends to put people back at the centre of developmental thinking. Along with the traditional goal of life sustenance, the human development paradigm advocates for dignity of all individuals in the society and most importantly freedom. Sen (1999) provides the broadest possible definition of development as expansion of freedom. The availability of choices or expansion of opportunities makes an individual free from illiteracy, ill-health, racial as well as ethnic discrimination, gender disparity etc. The role of every individual in decision making has been emphasized in such a manner that everybody recognizes his or her presence in development process. Freedom of different types has been viewed not only as the primary ends of development; they are also described as one of its principal means. The Human Development Index (HDI) has been formulated to capture the level of achievements of a society in terms of income, education and health. The exercise is often described as the Operationalisation of Sen's Capability Approach. This is a measure of achievements of a society in capability building. However, the formulation if often accused of being a mean of means. The national/state/district level averages seem to mask the existing disparities within the nation/ state/district. Sometimes the real urges and national of the common people remain suppressed or missed out in the process of calculation of HDI. Several attempts have been made to capture the real picture of human well-being. NHDR (2001) is an example of such attempt. State Human Development Reports published jointly by UNDP and the relevant state Governments are mention worthy in this occasion. Human development is therefore, the combination of people's entitlement and attainment relating to education, health and livelihood. These three areas, taken together form the everyday experience of development for the people as individuals and as members of a community, state or nation. The concept of human development is a people-centred approach to development where the primary concern is enhancement of human well-being. Human development therefore corresponds to a holistic approach in the process of development.

The present chapter adopts a methodology in which Bodo people's perception on development and on the long-lasting Bodo movement is taken as the cornerstone of the entire analysis. Emphasis has been given on people's vision, rather on the mathematical calculation of HDI. The present methodology is inspired by that of the award-winning Chhattisgarh ki Jan Rapat (Chhattisgarh State Human Development Report: 2005). The primary aim is to capture the situation of Bodo people living in four districts under Bodoland Territorial Area District (BTAD) from their own perceptions and analyses, and also to draw lines of thinking on the basis of majority perception. The primary information have been gathered from 300 households, taking three blocks each from all four districts under the jurisdiction of BTAD.

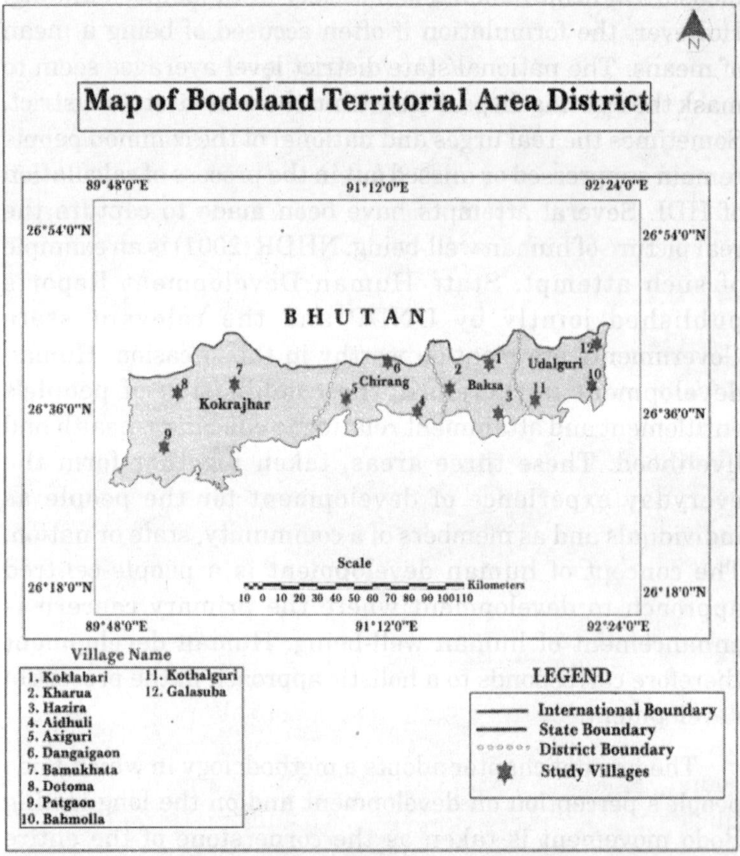

Map 5.1: Study Villages at a Glance

Study Villages: An Introduction through Secondary Sources

The following information is presented through secondary sources covering all four districts of Bodoland Territorial Area District and all information is covered by the primary survey and the location of sample villages selected at random for this research study is displayed in Map: 5.1. Twelve villages, located in twelve different blocks, give ample diversity in terms of geography, topography, access to modern facilities and other basic amenities. Some of our sample villages are remotely located in regard to their distances from the sub-divisional headquarters. The size of the sample villages in terms of the number of households varies significantly between 49 in Patgaon to 379 in Koklábari village. Accordingly, the total population varies between 275 in Patgaon and 2427 in Koklabari.

Koklabari

Koklabari is situated in the western part of the subdivision at 15 kilometers away from the Headquarter, Mosalpur. It is surrounded by other villages, mostly inhabited by Boros; the village is inhabited by the people of Boro community, which belongs to the constitutionally classified Scheduled Tribe category. The people of this village are the believers in Hindunised Bathou. The infrastructure facilities of the village are not so poor. This village is connected to other parts of the area by an un-graveled kutcha road and no.152 national highway is running nearby this village which is very attached to the said village in the west. The mode of transport of the village is mainly bicycle. The people of this village have to travel 1 kilometer south to reach to get a bus stand, and around 29 kilometers south to reach a railway station. The village has 3 Lower Primary schools and one middle school. The students of class VIII to X standards have to travel 1 kilometer either on-foot or by bicycle to reach their school. For the Higher Education, students have to go to K.C. College through no. 152 national highways with either by Bus or Bicycle near to village at Hazua, which is just about 1 kilometer from the village. B.B. Kishan College, another higher institution situated at Jalah under Jalah Development Block which is 7 kilometers from the village. People of this village give much emphasis on schooling of their children and send them to various educational institutions. According to Census 2001, total number of households was 379 with total population of the village 2427 of which 1215 male and 1212 female population. The Population of within 0-6 age-groups was 348 with 176 male and 172 female accounting about 14.33 per cent of total population. The overall literacy rate was recorded as 58.3 per cent, with about 72 per cent male literacy and 44.6 per cent female literacy. There was a sharp literacy gap of 27.4 per cent. Total number of working population constitutes 55.36 per cent and non worker constitutes 44.64 per cent. Main workers constitute 74.32 per cent and marginal workers are 25.68 per cent.

Kharua

Kharua is situated at the eastern boundary of Mosalpur Subdivision. It lies at around 2 kilometers east of the sub-divisional headquarters, and 5 kilometers north of the national highway no 31. It is also a big village and total number of households of the village was 391, with a total population of 2331 of which 1190 male and 1141 female population. Bodos constitute 93 per cent of total households in the village. Population composition in the village shows that 14.15 per cent of total population belongs to the age group (0-6), with a total number of 330 children of which 172 male and 158 female. Total literacy rate was recorded as 62.15 per cent in the village where male literacy rate was 71.6 per cent and female literacy rate was 52.7 per cent. Hence, the literacy gap was 18.9 per cent. The village has one LP School and one Middle School. There were 363 households in the village with a total population of 2331. The people of this village are the believers of Hinduism. Total working population in the village, according to the Census 2001, constitutes 52.76 per cent of total village population with 47.24 per cent non-workers. The main workers constitute 73.33 per cent of the total working population and marginal workers are 26.67 per cent. The infrastructure facilities in the village Kharrua is not impressive as compared to Koklabari in many respects. The village is situated 5 kilometers away from the NH-31, and is partially electrified. People had to travel 1 kilometer to reach the market and 5 kilometers to bank. The bus stop is also at 5 kilometers away from the village. The railway station is located at a distance of 32 kilometers. The common modes of transport of the people of this village are bus and bicycle.

Hazira

The village Hazira is situated 5 kilometers away from the sub-divisional headquarters in the south-eastern corner. The inhabitants are fully Bodos. Total number of households of the village was recorded in Census 2001 as 132 with a total population of 672 of which 343 male and 329 female. The overall literacy rate of the village was as poor as 41.8 per cent with 49.2 per cent male literacy and 34.4 per cent female literacy. The total workers in the village constitute 57.32 per cent of total population, leaving 42.68 per cent as non-worker. Main workers constitute 71.63 per cent and marginal workers 28.37 per cent of total working population. A large portion of population i.e. 51.15 per cent of the total working population is engaged in agriculture. The approach to the village is through a PWD road, passing all along the village from south to north direction. This was a motorable road 20 years ago. As all the bridges on the road are in miserable conditions, no vehicle today can move practically. The village has a lower primary school. The students of high school need to travel 3 kms, while college students 5 kilometers to reach Athiabari. The marketing facility, postal & banking services are also available at 5-kilometers away. The principal mode of transport is bicycle.

Aidhuli

The village Aidhuli is situated at about half kilometers east of Bijni subdivision headquarters. All the inhabitants of this village belong to Bodo community. They are followers of both Christian and Hindu faiths. This is the second smallest village among the 12 villages selected for primary survey. According to Census 2001, the total number household of the village is 53 with 97 per cent households belonging to the Bodo community, and the rest are of general category. The total population of the village was recorded as 276 with 148 male and 128 female. The literacy rate of the village is 59.35 per cent accounting 73.2 for male and 45.5 for female. Total working population in the village was 58.73 per cent and non workers constituted 41.27 per cent. Out of the total working population, main workers constituted 64.86 per cent and marginal workers are 35.14 per cent. This village enjoys a moderate level of infrastructure facilities. There are at least three approaches to the village from Bijni town. However, the village is not electrified. Different facilities, like banking, marketing, postal, telecommunication, education, railway, roadway, etc. are available at the nearby Bijni town, situated at a distance of just half a kilometer from the village. This is the village in which the highest per centage of the working population is engaged in the primary sector and the highest per centage in the tertiary sector, among all the 12 selected villages in spite of having all infrastructure facilities.

Axiguri

The village Axiguri is situated some 7 kilometers away from the sub-divisional headquarters, in the south-eastern part of Bijni sub-division. This village is relatively smaller than other two villages surveyed in Baksa District. It has 221 households with a total population of 1119. The male population was 599 and female 520, according to Census 2001. The most of the inhabitants of the village are Bodos as they constitute 93 per cent of total households. The people of the village believe in Hinduism. Total literacy rate was 54.7 per cent in the village. Male literacy rate was 63.8 per cent and female literacy rate was 45.6 per cent, the male-female literacy gap was 18.12 per cent. The total worker of the village was 56.31 per cent and non-worker was 43.69 per cent. Around 72.98 per cent of the total working force is reported as main workers while the rest 27.02 per cent as marginal workers.

Dangaigaon

Dangaigaon is a medium size village. It is situated at about 9 kilometers away from the sub-divisional headquarters, in the southeastern part of the subdivision. The number of households in the village was 96, with a total population of 485 as per 2001. Male population was 252 and female population 233. The overall literacy rate of the village was 60.3 per cent where male literacy rate was 70.8 per cent and female literacy rate was 49.8 per cent. There was male-female literacy gap of 21.1 per cent in the village. Total working population in the village constitutes 57.22 per cent of total population and non-workers 42.78 per cent. Around 79.45 per cent of total working population was reported as main workers and the rest 20.5 per cent werc marginal workers. The village has one LP school and one middle school. People of this village are the believers in Hindu religion. This village lies at 9 kilometers south of the NH- 31, running through the east-west direction. The village has a *Pucca* road on its northern part too. This road connects the village to the national highway. But the roads inside the village are un-graveled *kaccha* ones and are in miserable condition. There is a weekly market at a place called Boro bazar, which is situated at a distance of half kilometer from the village. This market is well known for vegetables.

Bamukhata

Bamukhata village is situated at around 13 kilometers away from the sub-divisional headquarters, in the southeastern part of Kokrajhar Sub-division. Most of the inhabitants of the village are Bodos. The main approach to the village is a kaccha road. The village possesses a primary school. The villagers have to travel about 5 kilometers to reach the nearest high school and to avail postal & banking services, marketing facility, healthcare, and to reach the nearest bus stop. The village is not yet fully electrified. According to Census 2001, total number of households of the village was 119 with a population of 601 of which male population was 298 and female population 303. 95 per cent of the total households belong to the Bodo community. The working population constitutes 55.38 per cent of the total population. Out of the total working population 60.53 per cent recorded as main workers and 39.47 per cent marginal workers. They work mainly in the agricultural sector. Among the total working population 81.89 per cent is engaged in the primary sector, of which 71.92 per cent is engaged in agriculture Literacy rate of the village was 59.1 per cent with male literacy 72 per cent and female literacy 46.2 per cent.

Dotoma

The village, Dotoma is situated at just 3 kilometers west of Kokrajhar sub-divisional headquarters. All the inhabitants of this village belong to Bodo community. They believe in Christianity. Because of the nearness to the Subdivision Headquarters, this village enjoys almost all the available infrastructure facilities. Different facilities, like banking, marketing, postal, telecommunication, education, railway, roadway, etc. are available at the nearby Dotoma town, which is situated at a distance of just 1 kilometer from the village. As per 2001 Census, total number of households in the village was only 87 with total population of 477 of which male population is 241 and female population is 236. Male literacy rate in the village stands at 72.8 per cent and female literacy rate constitutes 52.3 per cent. There seems male-female literacy gap of 20.5 per cent in the village. Within the village area, it has two LP schools and one High school. Total working population as per 2001 census, constitutes 53.22 per cent and non workers are 46.78 per cent where around 61.45 per cent engaged in agricultural cultivation. Main workers are 79.85 per cent and marginal farmers are 20.15 per cent.

Table 5.1
Study villages at a glance: secondary sources

Village	Block	Sub-Division	District	Dist. From SHQ (Km.)	No. of House-Holds (2001)	Population (Census 2001)		
						M	F	T
1	2	3	4	5	6	7	8	9
1. Koklabari	Jalah	Mosalpur	Baksa	15	379	1215	1212	2427
2. Kharua	Barama			5	391	1190	1141	2331
3. Hazira	Mosalpur			5	132	343	329	672
4. Aidhuli	Sidli Bijni	Chirang	.5	53	148	128	276	
5. Axiguri	Borobazar			7	221	599	520	1119
6. Dangaigaon	Manigpur			9	96	252	233	485
7. Bamunkhata	Gosaigaon	Kokrajhar	Kokrajhar	13	119	298	303	601
8. Dotama	Dotama			3	87	241	236	477
9. Patgaon	Titaguri			12	49	141	134	275
10. Bahmolla	Koirabari	Bhergaon	Udalguri	12	63	201	194	395
11. Khathalguri	Udalguri			9	95	297	280	577
12. Galasuba	Bhergaon			12	127	367	373	740

Table: 5.1. Continued

Village	*ST Pop. (%)*	*Working Population (% of Total Population)*		*Structure of Working Population (% of Total Workers)*		*Literacy Rate (%)(Census 2001)*		
		Workers	*Non-Workers*	*Main*	*Marginal*	*M*	*F*	*T*
1	*2*	*3*	*4*	*5*	*6*	*7*	*8*	*9*
1.Koklabari	100	53.74	46.26	74.32	25.68	72.00	44.6	58.3
2. Kharua	93	55.36	44.64	73.33	26.67	71.6	52.5	62.15
3. Hazira	100	51.25	48.75	71.63	28.37	49.2	34.4	59.35
4. Aidhuli	97	58.73	41.27	64.86	35.14	73.2	45.5	54.7
5. Axiguri	93	56.31	43.69	72.98	27.02	63.8	45.6	60.3
6. Dangaigaon	100	57.22	42.78	79.45	20.5	70.8	49.8	59.1
7.Bamunkhata	95	55.38	44.62	60.53	39.47	72.0	46.2	62.55
8. Dotama	100	53.22	46.78	79.85	20.15	72.8	52.3	54.6
9. Patgaon	94	55.51	44.49	72.31	27.69	68.1	41.1	60.01
10. Bahmolla	91	50.27	49.73	73.19	26.81	73.09	53.12	57.5
11.Khathalguri	93	57.10	42.9	78.36	21.64	64.02	51.56	55.9
12. Galasuba	100	51.20	48.8	77.11	22.89	64.8	46.10	

Source: Census of India-2001: Economic Tables, B-Series, Assam. BTC-report 2005.

Patgaon

Patgaon is the smallest amongst all the 12 villages for primary survey. It is situated at around 12 kilometers away from the sub-divisional headquarters in the southeastern part of the sub-division. The number of households in the village is 49 and its population is 275 with 141 male and 134 female. Out of the total households in the village 94 per cent households belong to the Bodo community. People of this village are the believers of both Christianity and Bathou religion. This village lies at 5 kilometers west of the national highway no-52 running in the north-south direction. The village has a *Pucca* road on its northern part too. This road connects the village to the national highway. But the roads inside the village are un-graveled *kaccha* ones and are in miserable condition. Working population constitutes 55.51 per cent of the total population, out of which 72.31 per cent are main workers and marginal workers constitute of 27.69 per cent.

Bahmulla

Bahmulla is situated at the eastern boundary of Bhergaon Subdivision. It lies at around 12 kilometers east of the sub-divisional head quarters, and 5 kilometers north of the National Highway No.37. It is a medium size village in which both Scheduled Tribe and General categories of people inhabit. There are 63 households in the village with total population of 395 out of which 91 per cent is the Bodo Population. Male population is recorded 201 while female population 194. Total literacy rate of the village is 64 per cent with 73.09 per cent male literacy and 53.12 per cent female literacy rate. The gender gap of literacy rate appears about 20.01 per cent. The people of this village are the believers of Hinduism. The infrastructure facilities of the village Bahmulla is worse-off. It is situated 12 kilometers away from the National Highroad No.37, there is a P.W.D. graveled

road passing through it. The village is not yet electrified and has weekly market. The bank, bus stop, railway station are all at a distance of 12 kilometers. The modes of transport of the people of this village are bus and bicycle.

Kothalguri

The village Kothalguri is situated 9 kilometers away from the sub-divisional headquarters in the north-western side. The inhabitants are tribal as well as general of communities. Though they are people of diverse communities and religious faiths, they have been living together for ages. A total of 577 populations are living in 95 households. Male population is 297 and female population is 280. Out of these 95 households, 88 households belong to Bodo community accounting 93 per cent of the total households of the village. Literacy rate of the village is 57.5 per cent while male literacy rate is 64.02 per cent and female literacy rate is 51.56 per cent as per 2001 census. The approach to the village is a PWD road passing through the south to north direction. This was a motorable road some 25 years ago. Now, motor vehicles cannot ply on this road, because all the bridges are in miserable condition. This village does not have power supply. The village has a lower primary school. The students of high school have to travel 3 kms, and college students about 5 kilometers for their higher education. The market, postal service as well as the banking facility are available at a 5-kilometers' distance. The principal mode of transport is bicycle.

Galasuba

Galasuba is the third biggest of all the 12 villages that have been selected for the primary survey. It is situated at around 12 kilometers away from the sub-divisional headquarters, in the south-eastern part of the sub-division. The number of households in the village is 127, and its population size is 740 with 367 male and 373 female populations. Literacy rate is 55.9 per cent where male literacy

rate is 64.8 per cent and female literacy rate is 46.10 per cent indicating a gap of 18.9 per cent. People of this village are the believers of Bathou religion. This village lies at 5 kilometers west of the NH-52, running through north-south direction. The village has a *pucca* road on its northern part too. This road connects the village to the national highway. But the roads inside the village are un-graveled *kaccha* ones and are in miserable condition. The total number of workers in village constitutes 51.20 per cent of the total population. The per centage of dependents is 49.80. The main workers constitute 77.11 per cent of the total working population and 22.89 per cent are marginal workers as per 2001 census.

Status of Human Development of Bodos: An Evaluation from Survey Data

Taking the stock of primary data, collected from 12 sample villages spread over all four Districts under Bodoland Territorial Area District, this section enumerates the level of human development that has been achieved by the Bodos living in Bodoland Territorial Area District. The methodology adopted in calculating human development index here has been similar to that of Assam Human Development Report 2003 so that a certain degree of comparability can be maintained.

Koklabari

As per the design of the study, twenty five sample households of the village have been surveyed for the study. The total population of the sample households is 148 of which male are 71 and female are 77 and the average family size is 5.92. The composition of population shows that there are 46 population below (0-6) years of which male children was 21 and female child was 25 respectively. But above six years population constitute 102 persons where male populations are 50 and female persons are 52 in numbers respectively. Above six years population constitutes 68.92 per cent. The infant mortality rate was 138 per thousand in the village which is very deplorable condition for the people in the village. Total 65 persons are literates, which account 43.92 per cent literacy rates in sample village, while male literacy rate constitutes 49.29 per cent and female literacy rate was 39.47 per cent. A significant part of income of the sample households comes from employment in government and non-governmental services, which contributes 50.51 per cent of the total income. The per centage share of income from agriculture is around 19.06 per cent of the total income. And the rest incomes are contributed (15.80 per cent) by labour and by Handloom and Handicraft (14.62 per cent). Per capita monthly income is Rs.1043 in the village.

The village Koklabari is partially electrified (28 per cent). Around 60 per cent sample households have their own Pucca houses and the rest populations have semi Pucca and Kutcha houses. Around 96 per cent sample households has their own safe drinking water facilities and about 88 per cent sample households had access to vaccination service facilities. Around 72 per cent households have sanitation facilities in the village and 96 per cent households have access to medical facilities and the rest households were unaware about it. Around 28 per cent sample household have electricity connection at their houses.

The residents have to go to Jalah, the block office of the said village to obtain banking services which is about 7 kilometer from the village. The post office is situated at village a distance of 1 kilometer in a nearby village. There is a small weekly market at a distance of half kilometer in which the people of the village can sale their merchandise like, paddy, vegetables and other household products, and purchase some necessary consumer goods. It is a small market place where people do not get all the necessary commodities for their consumption. They have to travel 1 kilometer to get proper market place and for medical treatment. Almost every household possesses its own well as a source of drinking water at a distance of half kilometer.

The women-folk of this village participate in many other activities, weaving, fishing, marketing, etc. Around 66.67 per cent of the households have their own weaving implements. They weave attires for themselves as well as for other members of the family and thereby reduce expenditures on these items. The women of this village also participate in many other economic activities, like rearing of cattle, pig, fouls, eri-worm, etc.; and some of them run small tea stalls in the weekly markets which also brings some income for the family. So, apart from keeping themselves busy in many household activities, the women of this village help the household in many other ways too.

The main crop in the village is paddy. The village cultivation depends exclusively on the Monsoon rain. There are no irrigation facilities available. There is no canal flowing through the agricultural lands of the village. Farmers can cultivate mainly the winter rice, like *Sali, Aijong, Ranjit, Laxman*, etc. and very few of them, having low-land, can cultivate the summer rice, called *Ahu* in the local parlance. The average productivity of paddy is 10 mounds per bigha. The so-called high yielding varieties (HYVs) of paddy covers an area of 211 bighas (39.91%) of the total of 528.7 bighas of area cultivated by the sample households. It is to be noted here, that these HYV seeds, which farmers use for cultivation, were introduced long back and people have been still using them on local exchange basis or by purchasing from local market. So, the high yielding capacity of these seeds has declined and they have become just like the ordinary traditional seeds. Besides paddy, farmers also cultivate other crops like jute, potato, tomato, cabbage, chili, ginger, etc. So, the village is out of reach of 'Mechanization' and 'Commercialization' of agriculture in the sense that farmers do not use any kind of machine in their paddy field and they produce crops to meet their yearly needs. Due to lack of proper marketing facility, farmers do not get satisfactory price for their produce. The price of paddy per quintal ranges from Rs. 250/- in the harvest season to Rs. 300/- in the peak price season. Most of the farmers in the village are not in a position to produce surplus of paddy. But, still then, they have to sell paddy at low harvest price to meet their farm maintenance cost, and have to purchase the same at high peak price to meet their consumption needs. Very few better-off farmers can wait for the peak price and receive comparatively satisfactory price for their produce.

Kharua

Kharua is situated at the eastern boundary of Mosalpur Subdivision. It lies at around 2 kilometers east of the Sub-divisional Head Quarters and 5 kilometers north of the national highway no. 31. A total of 25 sample households of the village have been surveyed for the study. It has been found that the average size of population of the village is 5.08. The literacy rate of the village is 48.03 per cent where male literacy rate is 57.75 per cent and female literacy rate is 35.71 per cent. The total number of population in the sample households is 127 of which male population are 71 and female are 56. Population of the (0-6) aged group constitutes only 18 persons in the sample households where male child was 11 and female children were only 7 in numbers respectively.

People of the village are engaged in different economic activities and they are to live the time favour. The primary sector activities are the dominant source of income and employment in the village. They still practice agricultural cultivation by a very old method, and farming is absolutely rain-fed. They use human and bullock powers in their farming. The main implements used in farming are wooden plough with iron ploughshare, iron-hoe with bamboo handle, sickle, etc. which are made in a very old and traditional

Table 5.2
Human development indicators: evidences from primary survey

Village / District	*Population*			*Average Family Size*			*Population of Below 6*		
	M	*F*	*T*	*M*	*F*	*T*	*M*	*F*	*T*
1. Koklabari	71	77	148	2.84	3.04	5.92	21	25	46
2. Kharua	71	56	127	2.84	2.24	5.08	11	7	18
3. Hazira	65	57	122	2.6	2.28	4.88	3	0	3
Baksa	207	190	397	2.76	2.5	5.3	35	32	67
4. Aidhuli	68	73	141	2.72	2.92	5.64	7	3	10
5. Axiguri	61	66	127	2.44	2.64	5.08	5	1	6
6. Dangaigaon	68	59	127	2.72	2.36	5.08	5	4	9
Chirang	197	198	395	2.62	2.6	5.3	17	8	25
7. Bamukhata	63	67	130	2.52	2.68	5.2	8	6	14
8. Dotoma	74	62	136	2.96	2.48	5.44	3	1	4
9. Patgaon	68	57	125	2.72	2.28	5	1	6	7
Kokrajhar	205	186	391	2.73	2.5	5.2	12	13	25
10. Bahmolla	70	74	144	2.8	2.96	5.76	4	3	7
11. Kothalguri	72	76	148	2.88	3.04	5.92	10	7	17
12. Galasuba	64	68	132	2.56	2.72	5.28	5	5	10
Udalguri	206	218	424	2.75	2.9	5.7	19	15	34
Total of 12 villages	815	792	1607	2.72	2.64	5.36	83	68	151

Source: Primary Survey

Table 5.3
Human development indicators

Village / District	*Literacy Rate (%)*			*Household Amenities (%)*					
	M	*F*	*T*	*PH*	*DW*	*SF*	*MF*	*CTV*	*EAH*
1. Koklabari	49.29	39.47	43.92	60	96	72	96	88	28
2. Kharua	57.75	35.71	48.03	8	96	12	96	20	36
3. Hazira	60.00	50.88	55.74	32	96	28	96	88	32
Baksa	57.21	41.58	48.87	33.33	96	37.33	96	65.33	32
4.Aidhuli	52.94	53.42	53.19	36	96	80	96	96	8
5. Axiguri	49.18	53.03	51.18	28	96	32	96	96	36
6. Dangaigaon	60.29	52.54	56.69	24	96	32	96	96	40
Chirang	54.31	53.03	53.67	29.33	96	48	96	96	28
7. Bamukhata	53.97	55.22	54.61	64	96	72	96	92	76
8. Dotoma	55.40	53.22	54.41	76	88	72	96	96	92
9. Patgaon	70.58	47.37	60.00	56	92	76	92	88	72
Kokrajhar	60.00	52.15	56.26	65.33	92	73.33	94.66	92	80
10.Bahmolla	51.43	48.65	50.00	24	92	40	96	88	0
11. Kothalguri	47.22	44.74	45.94	40	96	64	96	96	28
12. Galasuba	54.68	50.00	52.27	20	88	24	72	72	0
Udalguri	50.97	47.71	49.29	28	92	42.66	88	85.33	9.33
Total of 12 villages	55.21	48.61	51.96	39.0	94.0	50.33	93.67	84.67	37.33

Source: Primary Survey Notes: PH=Pucca House, DW=Drinking Water, SF=Sanitation Facilities, MF=Medical Facilities, CTV=Children Taken to Vaccination, EAH=Electricity at Home

Table 5.4
Human development indicators

Village / District	*Source of Household Income (Rs. at current prices / month)*					*Source of HouseholdIncome (%)*			
	IFS	*IFA*	*IFL*	*IHH*	*Total*	*IFS*	*IFA*	*IFL*	*IHH*
1. Koklabari	78000	29440	24400	22576	154416	50.51	19.06	15.80	14.62
2. Kharua	57000	28850	34824	27100	147774	38.57	19.52	23.56	18.39
3. Hazira	59000	29920	16000	22500	127420	46.30	23.48	12.55	17.66
Baksa	194000	88210	75224	72176	429610	45.16	20.53	17.51	16.80
4. Aidhuli	62500	24260	21900	11750	120410	51.90	20.14	18.18	9.76
5. Axiguri	77500	24090	19600	15120	136310	56.86	17.67	14.37	11.09
6. Dangaigaon	75500	25250	18750	13730	133230	56.66	18.95	14.07	10.30
Chirang	215500	73600	60250	40600	389950	55.26	18.87	15.45	10.41
7. Bamukhata	136500	25010	5550	11700	178760	76.35	13.99	3.10	6.54
8. Dotoma	143000	24960	8900	15900	192760	74.18	12.94	4.62	8.24
9. Patgaon	82933	22794	9128	15915	130030	63.78	17.53	7.02	12.24
Kokrajhar	362433	72704	23578	43515	501550	72.26	14.49	4.70	8.68
10. Bahmolla	35500	29060	22400	11050	100010	35.49	29.05	22.39	110.5
11. Kothalguri	161000	22790	17100	13800	214690	47.99	10.61	7.96	6.42
12. Galasuba	63000	22790	16500	12900	115190	54.69	19.78	14.33	11.20
Udalguri	259500	76440	56000	37750	429890	60.36	17.78	13.02	8.78
Total	1031433	309214	215052	194041	1943781	53.06	15.91	11.06	9.98

Source: Primary Survey Note: IFS=Income from Service, IFA=Income from Agriculture, IFL=Income from Labor, IHH=Income from handloom and handicraft

manner. As many as 13.33 per cent of the households possess trolley and about 10.00 per cent households have bullock carts, which they use as means of transportation for their crops and merchandise. Machines, manures, chemical fertilizers and pesticides, etc. are scantily used in the village. This is due to ignorance of the farmers, and in certain cases, due to lack of capital with the farmers. It may be noted that while in Koklabari use of fertilizers and pesticides is feared as it is believed to affect soil fertility adversely in the long run, the farmers of Kharua do not use these inputs on account of ignorance and lack of investible capital.

A significant part of income of the sample households comes from employment in government and non-governmental services, which contributes 38.57 per cent of the total income. The per centage share of income from agriculture is around 19.52 per cent of the total income. And the rest incomes are contributed (23.56 per cent) by labour and by Handloom and Handicraft (18.39 per cent). Though saving structure has not been assessed in the survey of sample village, yet, low level saving situation has prevailed among the people of the village and this circumstances led them to borrow during summer when crisis occurred. Sometimes, hiring of labourers, both male and female, is prevalent in the village. Labour is hired on contractual basis. The reasons for hiring of labour in cultivation are the same as that of the previous village (Koklabari). But unlike in Koklabari village where labour payments are made in kinds, wages of the labourers in this village are paid mostly in cash. Moreover, they find it uneconomical to hire labourers on yearly basis, because the season of cultivation for most of the farmers lasts for 6 months only. Moreover, there is an abundant supply of wage labourers from the village.

Therefore, the farmers need to hire some labourers on daily, monthly and on contractual basis. All labourers are demanded for agricultural cultivation. The hired labourers are engaged in the same activities as were found in the first village. Wages of labourers hired on monthly basis ranges from Rs.700 to Rs.1200 per month, depending on the same principle of age, working capability and experience of the worker. Hired labourers get their food and lodging in their master's house. Inclusive of their food, lodging and other facilities getting from the master, the daily wage rate of a monthly-ploughman amounts to Rs.70. The daily wage rate of the ploughman is fixed at Rs.80. Working hour of a daily-ploughman is five hours a day. Hiring of daily and contractual labourer is very significant, for uprooting of plants from the nursery and for harvesting the crops.

There is some form of division of labour on the basis of gender as regards agricultural cultivation is concerned. The ploughing of agricultural fields is exclusively the job of the men folk. The act of plant transferring from the seedbed, where the seed is sown, is also done by the male-folk. But work of transplantation of paddy is taken care of by both men and women in this village. In some households, which are unable to resort to hiring of labour, both male and female workers of the family join hands in harvesting their crops. While cooking is the primary duty of the women, men take the principal responsibility of raising crops from the agricultural fields. But when more labourers are urgently required, women also participate in harvesting. Ploughing the agricultural field and uprooting of plants from the nursery are exclusive jobs of men in this village. Earlier, women used to do the husking in the household itself with the help of what is called *'dheki'* or *'dingkhi'* (a wooden implement for husking paddy into rice) in the local parlance. But nowadays, mini rice mills (husking) have become available in the village. So, in most of the cases now, unless some unavoidable circumstances occur, men do this job by carrying it to mills.

Moreover, the women-folk of this village too keep themselves busy in many other activities like weaving, fishing, marketing, etc. Around 32.33 per cent of the households have their own weaving implements. They make attires for themselves as well as for other members of the family and thus, reduce expenditures on these items. As a household industry, women of some families of the village also undertake weaving on commercial basis. Women of the poorer families make rice-beer on commercial basis. Though it is a forbidden activity, they go in for it because it is highly profitable. Almost every household rears cattle, fouls, pig etc., which fetches some per cent of their income.

As per our village survey report, around 8 per cent of sample households have their own Pucca houses and about 37 per cent of the sample households have semi Pucca houses. And the rest are having Kutcha houses. Almost 96 sample family or household has their own safe drinking water facilities and has access to medical facilities. Around 20 per cent sample households were having vaccination facilities and 12 per cent households have sanitation facilities in the village. 36 per cent households have electricity connection at their houses in the village which was comparatively advanced than the previous village, Koklabari.

Hazira

The village Hazira is situated 5 kilometers away from the sub divisional Headquarters in the south- eastern side. The inhabitants are Boros. As per the sample survey of 25 households, total number of population was 122 of which male population was 65 and female population was 57, the average household size of the village is 4.88 persons. Total population of the sample household of the age group of (0-6) is found to be only 3 persons. Adult populations which are the people of above six onwards constitute 119 persons in the sample village which accounts 97.54 per cent. The literacy rate of the village is 55.74 per cent where male literacy rate was 60.0 per cent and female literacy rate was 50.88 per cent. The village has a lower primary school. The students of high school have to travel 3 kms and college level students have to go to Athiabari situated at a distance of 5 kilometers, for their higher education. The marketing facility, postal service, etc. are also available at a 5-kilometers' distance, as well as the banking facility is available at a distance of 5 kilometers. The principal mode of transport is 'bicycle'.

The majority of people of this village depend on agriculture. Their practice of farming is based on very old and out-dated method. Farmers use human and bullock power to raise their crops. On rare occasions, when a farmer does not possess bullocks, a machine, like a hired tractor, is used for ploughing. Farming in the village is absolutely rain-fed. As soon as the monsoon rain starts pouring, farmers begin to put dams on the small rivers to raise water in their agricultural fields. Paddy is their principal crop. They cultivate different varieties of paddy, like, *aijong, ranjit, masuri, pankaj,* etc. But, due to very old and traditional farming method, these varieties also have no significant advantage in productivity vis-à-vis the more traditional/local varieties. The productivity of paddy in this village ranges from 8 to 10 mounds per bigha, depending on seasonal fluctuations and position (high or low) of the land.

About 32 per cent of sample households have their own Pucca houses and the rest households of the sample village have either their semi-Pucca houses or Kutcha houses. Regarding safe drinking water, around 96 per cent sample households have their own safe drinking water and around 28 per cent of sample households have sanitation facilities and only 4 per cent sample household does not have access to medical facilities because of their unawareness.. Around 88 per cent sample household has access to vaccination services and around 32 per cent of sample households have electricity connection at their house. However, a significant part of income of the sample households comes from employment in government and non-government services, which contributes 46.30 per cent of the total income. The per centage share of income from agriculture is around 23.48 per cent of the total income. The rest of incomes are contributed, respectively, by labour (12.55) per cent and income from Handloom and Handicraft is around 17.66 per cent of the total income. With regards to division of labour, the same system is prevalent here as that of previous villages. Apart from helping men in the agricultural fields, women of this village take very active part in other economic activities like animal husbandry (rearing cattle, foul and pig) raising eri-worm and weaving, fishing, etc.

Aidhuli

The village Aidhuli is situated at 1 kilometer east of Bijni Subdivision Head Quarters. All the inhabitants of this village belong to Bodo community. They believe both in Christian and Hindu religion. People of the village have various infrastructure facilities nearby sub divisional office. They had to travel only around one kilometer distance to avail facilities like school, public health center, market place, post office and bus stop. Road condition is also good to approach to the village. A total of 25 sample households were randomly surveyed for the study. The total population of the sample households is 141 and the average size of the household is 5.64 persons. Populations below six years are only 10 in number in the sample village. This village has a literacy rate of 53.19 per cent where male literacy rate was 52.94 per cent and female literacy rate was 53.42 per cent, which is the second highest among all the three villages of Baksa districts surveyed for the study. People of the village also are engaged in different economic activities. The primary sector activities are the dominant source of income and employment in the village. They also still practice agricultural cultivation by a very old method, and farming is absolutely rainfed. They use human and bullock powers in their farming. The main implements used in farming are wooden plough with iron ploughshare, iron-hoe with bamboo handle, sickle, etc. which are made in a very old and traditional manner. Machines, manures, chemical fertilizers and pesticides, etc. are scantily used in the village. This is due to ignorance of the farmers, and in certain cases, due to lack of capital with the farmers. People of the village could not develop themselves in various aspects though they are living nearby semi town. People even today believe in traditional way of thinking and they also not realized modern method of human living. About 36 per cent of surveyed households have Pucca houses, 96 per cent have own source of safe drinking water facilities. Around 96 per cent sample households were having vaccination facilities and 80 per cent households have sanitation facilities in the village, but only 8 per cent sample household have electricity connection at their house. The services sector contributes the highest amount of income to the economy of the village constituting 51.90 per cent of the total income of the sample households. Because of nearness to the town, the village gets more education facilities, leading to more educated persons as well as higher number of service holders in both governmental and non-government institutions. This sector is followed by the agricultural sector, which contributes 20.14 per cent of its income. Agriculture contributes around 20.14 per cent and labour contributes 18.18 per cent of the total income of the sample households. The rest of income accrues from handloom and handicraft (9.76 per cent).

The institution of hiring labour is very prominent in this village. The main reason for this is that most of the farming households have their members engaged in various non-agricultural employments. They cannot participate in agricultural activities fully. Therefore, these households must resort to hiring of labour. The existing wage rate of daily labourer is Rs.70 per day for the ploughman and other manual workers, and Rs. 45 for transplantation by female labourers.

And, depending on sex, age and experience, the wage rate of monthly labour ranges from Rs. 700 to Rs. 900 per month. The division of labour in this village is also the same as that of Kharua and Hazira. Apart from household activities, participation of women in various economic activities such as agriculture, weaving, rearing of cattle, pig, foul, and marketing, etc. is remarkable.

Axiguri

The village Axiguri is situated some 7 kilometers away from the sub-divisional Headquarters, in the southeastern part of Bijni Subdivision. This village is relatively smaller than the first two villages which have been presented earlier in Baksa district and bigger than Aidhuli village of the same district as we have come across so far. There is link road from village to small market place in front of the village and this link road leads to reach national highway no- 31. For primary education or schooling students of the village Axiguri has to travel one kilometer distance as well as for public health center. For market place they had to travel at least two kilometers where other facilities like post office and bus stop can be reached. The national highway no.31 passes through the western part of the village in the North-South direction. A kuchha road connects the village with the highway. The village has partial electricity facility. It receives marketing facility, regional rural banking facility, postal service facility, high school education facility, etc. from a small town, called Dalgaon town, situated at a distance of less than 2 kilometers from the village.

A sample survey was conducted in 25 households. The total population of these households is 127 the average household size being 5.08 persons, and literacy rate 51.18 per cent. Where male literacy rate was 49.18 per cent and female literacy rate was 53.03 per cent respectively. The village has more female literate persons. People of the village engaged in various economic activities and likewise they earn their livelihood. Income from the service activities contributes 56.86 per cent of the total income. The per centage share of income from agriculture is around 17.67 per cent of the total income. The rest of incomes are contributed, respectively, by labour (14.37) per cent and income from Handloom and Handicraft is around 11.09 per cent of the total income. Not only have these, people of the sample village accrued income from various sources also.

About 28 per cent of sample households have their own Pucca houses and 37 per cent households have their semi-Pucca houses and 35 per cent sample households had kuchha houses. Regarding safe drinking water, around 96 per cent sample households have their own safe drinking water. Around 32 per cent only sample households have sanitation facilities. More than 95 sample households have access to vaccination services and around 36 per cent of sample households have electricity connection at their house. The infant mortality rate was 77 per thousand in the village which was less than the infant mortality rates of the previous village like Koklabari, Kharua in Baksa district and Aidhuli in the same district.

Dangaigaon

It is situated at around 9 kilometers away from the sub-divisional Head Quarters, in the southeastern part of the subdivision. This village is partially electrified, only 10 per cent of the sample households have electricity connection at their houses. The postal service, high school education, bus stoppage, telephone facility, etc. are obtainable from Dangaigaon semi town. For banking service, college education, etc., the villagers have to travel some 3 kilometers. A sample survey was conducted in 25 households. The total population of these households is 127 of which male was 68 and female was 59, the average household size being 5.08

persons, and literacy rate 56.69 per cent where male literacy rate was 60.29 per cent and female literacy rate was 52.54 per cent.

Agriculture is the main stay of the people of the village. The farmers of this village have used several modern technologies in the field of agriculture. Most of them use tractors in their agricultural fields instead of bullock powers. They adopt multiple cropping patterns raising three to four crops, especially *rabi* crops, in a year on the same plot of land. On the contrary to what we have found in the first five villages where farmers are hesitant in using chemical fertilizers and pesticides, the farmers of this village use almost all possible inputs in the cultivation of various crops. The farmers of this village are more interested in the HYV seeds of vegetable and cash crops. They put every necessary labour and care into raising the maximum possible output from these crops. The middle and big farmers do capitalistic type of farming, using huge investment of capital on seeds, machines, hired labours, etc., producing surplus for sale and exhibiting profit motive to farming. If we analyze generation of income from various activities it has been found that the services contribute 56.66 per cent of the total income. Agriculture contributes (18.95 per cent), from manual labours (14.07 per cent) and handloom and handicraft contributes (10.30 per cent. About 24 per cent of sample households have their own Pucca houses and 42 per cent households have their semi-Pucca houses and 34 per cent sample households had Kuchha houses. Regarding safe drinking water, around 96 per cent households have their own safe drinking water facilities and 96 per cent households have medical facilities as well as vaccination services. Around 32 per cent of sample households have sanitation facilities whereas only 40 per cent sample households have electricity connection at their house.

Bamukhata

Out of 119 households in the village, a total of 25 sample

households were randomly surveyed for the study. The total population of the sample households is 130, and the average size of the household is 5.2 persons. This village has a literacy rate of 54.61 per cent where male literacy rate was 53.97 per cent and female literacy rate was 55.22 per cent.

Service and agriculture are the main occupation of the village. Around 60 per cent household or family has at least one service holder in the village. The services sector contributes the highest amount of income to the economy of the village constituting 76.35 per cent of the total income of the sample households. In spite of living far away from town, the village gets more education facilities, leading to more educated persons as well as higher number of service holders in both governmental and non-governmental institutions. Not only this, farmers also engage themselves fully on cultivation of their own land and the produce consumes themselves rather than commercial purposes. This sector brings 13.99 per cent of the total income of the sample households. The small farmers, who do not possess enough cultivable land to work on their own land for the whole year, supply their services as part-time agricultural or other labourers. Paddy is the principal crop of the village. The farmers of the village cultivate *Boro*, which is a HYV paddy. The average yield of this variety of paddy ranges from 10 to 15 mounds per bigha. The other crops, cultivated in less quantity of area, are—jute, chili, vegetables, etc. Farmers get very little chance to cultivate *rabi* and *winter* crops because most of the cultivable lands remain submerged under water in these seasons. Their agricultural cultivation methods are a little developed than the first six villages we have come across so far, in the sense that, most of the farmers of the village use tractor, HYV seeds, manures, chemical fertilizers, pesticides, etc. They also adopt more meticulous practices, like timely use of manure, fertilizers, and weed clearing, etc. in cultivation than the farmers of those five villages.

Handloom and handicraft activities contribute 6.54 per cent of the total income of the sample households and around 3.10 per cent income accrues from manual labour. About 64 per cent of sample households have their own Pucca houses and 16 per cent households have their semi-Pucca houses and 20 per cent sample households had Kachha houses. Regarding safe drinking water and medical facilities are concerned around 96 per cent sample households were having their own safe drinking water and medical facilities. Around 72 per cent of sample households have sanitation facilities and with 92 per cent sample households has access to vaccination facilities and around 76 per cent of sample households have electricity connection at their house.

Dotoma

The village, Dotoma is situated at just 3 kilometers west of Kokrajhar Subdivision Head Quarters. All the inhabitants of this village belong to Bodo community. They believe in Christianity. Because of the nearness to the Subdivision Headquarters, this village enjoys almost all the available infrastructure facilities.. Different facilities, like banking, marketing, postal, telecommunication, education, railway, roadway, etc. are available at the nearby Dotoma town, which is situated at a distance of just 1 kilometer from the village.

A total of 25 sample households were randomly surveyed for the study. The total population of the sample households is 136, and the average size of the household is 5.44 persons. This village has a literacy rate of 54.41 per cent where male literacy rate is 55.40 per cent and female literacy rate is 53.22 per cent. The actual working population is only 48.58 per cent of the total sample population and 54.73 per cent of the total labour-force. Out of this, 64.86 per cent constitutes the main working population and 35.14 per cent, the marginal workers. A significant portion of the working population of the sample households is engaged in service sector and the services sector contributes the highest amount of income to the economy of the village constituting 74.18 per cent of the total income of the sample households. Because of nearness to the town, the village gets more education facilities, leading to more educated persons as well as higher number of service holders in both governmental and non-governmental institutions. This sector is followed by the agriculture contributes around 12.94 per cent. The second occupation of the people of the sample households is agriculture; around 33.24 per cent of the working population is directly or indirectly engaged in it. The agriculture of this village depends almost absolutely on rainfall. Farmers of this village can cultivate only the winter varieties of paddy, like, *aijong, ranjit, bora,* etc. All the cultivable land remains fallow during the rest of the cropping seasons. About 2.30 per cent of the working population is engaged as other labours. The rest of the working population is distributed among other activities. Handloom and handicraft contributes 8.24 per cent and manual labour contributes 4.62 per cent. Around 76 per cent of sample households have their own Pacca houses and 24 per cent households have their own kachcha houses. Regarding safe drinking water, about 88 per cent sample households have their own safe drinking water. Around 72 per cent of sample households have sanitation facilities. Only around 8 per cent sample households were not having electricity connection at their houses to be used for domestic purpose. The infant mortality rate in sample village is recorded to 78 where the same was only 58 in Bamukhata village of the same district as explained above.

Patgaon

Patgaon is the smallest of all the 12 villages that have been selected for the primary data collection. It is situated at around 12 kilometers away from the sub-divisional Head Quarters, in the southeastern part of the subdivision. A total of 25 sample households were randomly surveyed for the study. The total population of the sample households is 125, and the average size of the household is 5 persons. This village has a literacy rate of 60 per cent where male literacy rate is 70.58 per cent and female literacy rate is 47.37 per cent.

The actual working population in the sample household constitutes 50.31 per cent of the total population, out of which 70.53 per cent are main workers and marginal workers constitute of 29.47 per cent. The major portion of the working population 63.83% including agricultural labourers is, fully or partially, engaged in agricultural sector. Farmers of this locality give more emphasis on *Rabi* crops than *kharifs*. They utilize more than 60 per cent of the cultivated area in *Rabi* crops, mostly under vegetables like cabbage, cauliflower, brinjal, tomato, potato, radish, ladies finger, peas, gourds, corner gourd, chili, cucumber, carrot, beans, etc. During the *rabi* crop season selling and buying of these merchandise in bulk becomes an everyday affair. Varieties of vegetables are supplied to different parts of the state. But, even then, the farmers express their dissatisfaction with the existing prices of their produce, which, according to them, is very low. Most of the farmers cultivate paddy only for their household consumption.

The farmers of this village have used several modern technologies in the field of agriculture. Most of them use tractors in their agricultural fields instead of bullock powers. They adopt multiple cropping patterns raising three to four crops, especially *rabi* crops, in a year on the same plot of land. On the contrary to what we have found in the first five villages where farmers are hesitant in using chemical fertilizers and pesticides, the farmers of this village use almost all possible inputs in the cultivation of various crops. The farmers of this village are more interested in the HYV seeds of vegetable and cash crops. They put every necessary labour and care into raising the maximum possible output from these crops. The middle and big farmers do capitalistic type of farming, using huge investment of capital on seeds, machines, hired labours, etc., producing surplus for sale and exhibiting profit motive to farming. Most of them cultivate paddy only for household consumption. A significant portion of the working population of the sample households is engaged in service sector and the services sector contributes the highest amount of income to the economy of the village constituting 63.78 per cent of the total income of the sample households Because of nearness to the town, the village gets more education facilities, leading to more educated persons as well as higher number of service holders in both government and non-government institutions. This sector is followed by the agriculture contributes around 17.53 per cent. Other activities were also performed by the villagers likewise Handloom and handicraft contributes 12.24 per cent and manual labour contributes 7.02 per cent. The village Patgaon though far away from the subdivisional office, yet villagers can avail various infrastructure facilities nearby village market place where banking service, schooling, public health center, post service. bus stoppage etc are available just about one kilometer distance.

Our survey report shows that about 56 per cent of sample households have their own Pucca houses and the rest households have their either semi-Pucca houses or kachha houses. The sample households have access to medical facilities and have their safe drinking water both of which constitute around 92 per cent. Around 76 per cent of sample households have sanitation facilities and about 88 per cent sample households have access to vaccination facilities. The sample village though not fully electrified around 72 per cent sample households have electricity connection at their house. The infant mortality rate in the village was only 30 per thousand population which comparatively less than the previous villages.

Bahmulla

Bahmulla is situated at the eastern boundary of Bhergaon Subdivision. It lies at around 12 kilometers east of the Subdivisional Head Quarters and 5 kilometers north of the national highway no.37. It is a medium size village in which both Scheduled Tribe and General categories of people inhabit.

A total of 25 sample households of the village have been surveyed for the study. It has been found that the average size of population of the village is 5.76. The literacy rate of the village is 50 per cent. Male literacy rate is 51.43 per cent and female literacy rate is 48.64 per cent. Total population in the sample household was 144 out of which male was 70 and female was 74 persons. Female persons are more than the male persons in the sample household. Total literate persons are 72 out of the total population of 144 in the sample village. As it has been mentioned earlier, the majority of people of this village depend on agriculture. Their practice of farming is based on very old and out-dated method. Farmers use human and bullock power to raise their crops. On rare occasions, when a farmer does not possess bullocks, a machine, like a hired tractor, is used for ploughing. Farming in the village is absolutely rain-fed. As soon as the monsoon rain starts pouring, farmers begin to put dams on the small rivers to raise water in their agricultural fields. Paddy is their principal crop. They cultivate different varieties of paddy, like, aijong, ranjit, pankaj, ahu, sali, etc. But, due to very old and traditional farming method, these varieties also have no significant advantage in productivity vis-à-vis the more traditional/local varieties. The productivity of paddy in this village ranges from 10 to 12 mounds per bigha, depending on seasonal fluctuations and position of the land.

A few persons of the sample household engaged in govt. and non govt. departmental sector particularly in primary schools, police forces, etc and accordingly the services sector contributes the highest amount of income to the economy of the village constituting 35.49 per cent of the total income of the sample households. In spite of living far away from town, the village gets more education facilities, leading to more educated persons as well as higher number of service holders in both governmental and non-governmental institutions. This sector is followed by the agricultural sector, which contributes 29.05 per cent of its income. Manual labour contributes around 22.39 per cent and handloom and handicraft contributes 11.05 per cent of the total income of the sample households. About 24 per cent of sample households have their own Pucca houses and 26 per cent households have their semi-Pucca houses and the rest 50 per cent sample households had kachha houses. Around 92 per cent sample households have their own safe drinking water. Around 40 per cent of sample households have sanitation facilities and about 88 per cent sample households has access to vaccination facilities. No electricity connection to the village.

Kothalguri

The village Kothalguri is situated 9 kilometers away from the subdivisional Headquarters in the north-western side. The inhabitants are tribal as well as general of communities. The people tribal community is Hindus/ Christians and, those of the General category Hindus. Though they are people of diverse communities and religions, they have been living together for ages, except very minor differences in thoughts and actions.

As per the sample survey of 25 households, the average household size of the village is 5.92 persons. The literacy rate of the village is 45.94 per cent. Male literacy rate is 47.22 per cent and female literacy rate is 44.74 per cent. The dependent population amounts to 42.90 per cent. A large portion of population of the sample households is engaged in agriculture, which constitutes 51.15 per cent of the total working population, out of which 13.96 per cent constitutes the agricultural labourers. Other labourers constitute about 9.56 per cent of the total workers. The majority of people of this village depend on agriculture. Their practice of farming is based on very old and out-dated method. Farmers use human and bullock power to raise their crops. On rare occasions, when a farmer does not possess bullocks, a machine, like a hired tractor, is used for ploughing. Farming in the village is absolutely rain-fed. As soon as the monsoon rain starts pouring, farmers begin to put dams on the small rivers to raise water in their agricultural fields. Paddy is their principal crop. The services activities contribute around 47.99 per cent of the total income of the sample households. In this village also a few persons were engaged in different departmental either of govt. or semi govt. making themselves keeps earns their livelihood. This sector is followed by the agricultural sector, which contributes 10.61 per cent of its income. Manual labour contributes around 7.96 per cent and handloom and handicraft contributes 6.42 per cent of the total income of the sample households. The sample study reveals that about 40 per cent of sample households have their own Pucca houses and 16 per cent households have their semi-Pucca houses and 44 per cent sample households had kachha houses. Also about 96 per cent sample household have access to medical facilities. Whereas around 64 per cent only sample households have sanitation facilities and around 28 per cent sample household have electricity connection at their houses which indicates that majority sample households have to live without electricity power.

Galasuba

Galasuba is the third biggest of all the 12 villages that have been selected for the primary data collection. It is situated at around 12 kilometers away from the sub-divisional

Head Quarters, in the southeastern part of the subdivision. This village lies at 5 kilometers west of the national highway no.52 running in the north-south direction. The village has a *pucca* road on its northern part too. This road connects the village to the national highway. But the roads inside the village are un-graveled *kuchha* ones and are in miserable condition. A total of 25 sample households of the village have been surveyed for the study. It has been found that the average size of population of the village is 5.28. The literacy rate of the village is 52.27 per cent. Male literacy rate is 54.68 per cent and female literacy rate is 50 per cent. This village is not electrified. The postal service, high school education, bus stoppage, telephone facility, etc. are obtainable from Rumari chawk whish is around 3 kilometers from the village. For banking service, college education, etc., the villagers have to travel some 5 to 10 kilometers.

The economy of the villagers is not different from other villages so far we have discussed .the villagers also acts different economic activities to earn their livelihood. The village economy also depends on services sector, which contributes some amount of income to the economy of the village constituting 54.69 per cent of the total income of the sample households. This sector is followed by the agricultural sector, which contributes 19.78 per cent of its income. Manual labour contributes around 14.33 per cent and handloom and handicraft contributes 11.20 per cent of the total income of the sample households. The main crop in the village is paddy. The village cultivation depends exclusively on the Monsoon rain. There are no irrigation facilities available. There is no canal flowing through the agricultural lands of the village. Farmers can cultivate mainly the winter rice, like *Sali, Aijong, Ranjit, Laxman*, etc. and very few of them, having low-land, can cultivate the summer rice, called *Ahu* in the local parlance. The average productivity of paddy is 10 mounds per bigha. It is to be noted here, that HYV seeds, which farmers use for cultivation, were introduced long back and people have been still using them on local exchange basis or by purchasing from local market. So, the high yielding capacity of these seeds has declined and they have become just like the ordinary traditional seeds. Besides paddy, farmers also cultivate other crops like, jute, potato, tomato, cabbage, chili, ginger, etc.

Our survey reveals that around 20 per cent of sample households have their own Pucca houses and 24 per cent households have their semi-Pucca houses and 56 per cent sample households had kachha houses. Regarding safe drinking water, around 88 per cent sample households have their own safe drinking water and 72 per cent sample household have access to medical facilities. Only 24 per cent of sample households have sanitation facilities and 72 per cent sample households could avail vaccination facilities for children. The village is not electrified.

Evaluation of Human Development Index

This section uses the stock of primary information, discussed in the previous sections, to construct the composite index (HDI) for the sample villages separately. And adjusting them for the sample errors the district level as well as overall BTAD level is enumerated. The effort is to capture the status of human development for the Bodo people living in the area of our concern. The Human Development Index for the Bodos is calculated following the exact methodology adopted in estimating Assam Human Development Report 2003 so that a comprehensive comparison between the levels of human development of Bodos and overall state average can be made.

Table-5.5 displays the level of human development of Bodos living in BTAD. The Human Development Index and its decomposition by indices are displayed in Table: 5.5. As we have mentioned earlier that the survey work for the primary data collection has been conducted during the year 2003.Therefore, the direct comparison between two sets of values of HDI- first, for the state average obtained from Assam Human Development Report (2003) and second for the Bodos living in the areas under BTAD obtained from our primary survey during 2003 may be proper for practical purposes. First, we look at the indicator wise achievements of Human Development Index of Bodos obtained from primary survey. The overall Human Development Index of Bodos living in the areas under BTAD is as low as .426 which is defined as low human development level in UNDP literature. However, the average of BTAD seems to mask the variations across the districts and villages. For example, the district of Udalguri has emerged as highest scorer among all four districts under consideration -the district attains a level which is recognized as medium level of human development in the mainstream human development literature. Next comes the district of Kokrajhar which lags marginally behind the level of medium human development level. The remaining two districts of Baksa and Chirang are recorded very poor expansions of human development. Highest income attainment is recorded for the district of Kokrajhar, followed by Baksa. Udalguri emerges as best performer in one of the non-income attainments – health while Kokrajhar again stands tall in educational attainment. The other two districts namely, Baksa and Chirang are consistently poor performers in all three aspects of human capability.

A disturbing level of variations across the sample villages over all three attainments are found in our primary survey. The sample village that scores highest in the composite index of HDI is Patgaon in Kokrajhar, followed by Kothalguri and Galasuba in Udalguri district. These three villages in the list of twelve sample villages could only cross the .500 mark, considered as medium level. On the other end, Aidhuli in

Table 5.5
Human development index of Bodos: 2003

Village/District	*Literacy Rate (%)*	*Combined Enrolment Ratio*	*Education Index*	*Infant Mortality Rate*	*Health Index*	*PCNSDP (2007-08) Const. 93-94 prices*	*Income Index*	*HDI*
1. Koklabari	43.92	33.87	0.402	139	0.007	6260	0.299	0.236
2. Kharua	48.03	27.13	0.407	119	0.15	6981	0.351	0.303
3. Hazira	55.74	48.17	0.527	39	0.721	6266	0.299	0.516
Baksa	48.87	34.61	0.438	107	0.236	6493	0.352	0.342
4. Aidhuli	53.19	41.11	0.487	138	0.014	5123	0.204	0.235
5. Axiguri	51.18	37.89	0.463	83	0.407	6440	0.312	0.394
6. Dangaigaon	56.69	39.41	0.504	67	0.521	6294	0.301	0.442
Chirang	53.67	38.45	0.481	97	0.307	5923	0.273	0.354
7. Bamukhata	54.61	41.87	0.499	62	0.557	8251	0.429	0.495
8. Dotoma	54.41	39.56	0.45	84	0.4	8504	0.443	0.431
9. Patgaon	60	53.12	0.571	31	0.779	6241	0.297	0.549
Kokrajhar	56.26	47.11	0.527	63	0.55	7696	0.396	0.491
10. Bahmolla	50	41.55	0.467	35	0.75	4167	0.107	0.441
11. Kothalguri	45.94	33.56	0.414	43	0.693	8704	0.454	0.52
12. Galasuba	52.27	48.36	0.505	24	0.829	5236	0.214	0.516
Udalguri	49.29	42.33	0.465	35	0.75	6083	0.285	0.5
Total	51.96	39.99	0.475	79	0.436	7258	0.368	0.426

Source: Primary Survey.

Chirang and Koklabari in Baksa arte the poorest performers to achieve even the threshold of .300 mark of Human Development Index. Before entering into the conceptual comparison between Bodos and the state average of Assam we can record that there is unacceptable level of poor expansion of human development for the Bodo respondents living in the areas under BTAD.

A gross comparison of overall Human Development Index and its attainment-wise dimension indices are displayed in Figure 5.1 where between two calculations of HDI the comparison reveals that the value of overall human development index of Bodos obtained from primary data is found marginally higher than that of the State average. This can be justified by the argument that between two estimates the relevant indices of Bodo community living in the areas under BTAB has improved slightly. This observation does not apparently establish the spirit of our second hypothesis set in Chapter III. The decomposition of attainments in three dimensions, however, reveals a crucial picture. The income index for Bodos obtained from primary survey has been significantly higher than that of the state average obtained from the State Human Development Report while other two non-income dimensions, namely health and education are lagging significantly behind. The non-income components of Bodo Human Development Index from primary data are falling short to those of the state average indicates clearly there is a shortfall in the expansion of human capability in case of Bodos living in the areas under BTAD.

A very common weakness of the formulation of HDI is that any shortfall in educational or health attainment can be easily compensated by the brighter performance in income. Therefore, a further disaggregated comparison of indices between Bodos and State average of Assam will be more appropriate to explain the differences between the levels of human development. The analysis of relative contributions of three dimensions of Human Development Index to overall composite index has been able to focus on the present scenario. The relative contribution of each dimension of HDI, given by the formulation, $(\frac{I_j}{HDI}) \times 100$ Where, I_j = jth Dimension index for the economy and HDI = Overall Human Development Index for the economy, are calculated and displayed in the Figure: 5.2 for three categories of population:

- Five Bodo Districts of Assam
- State Average of Assam
- Bodos living in BTAD.

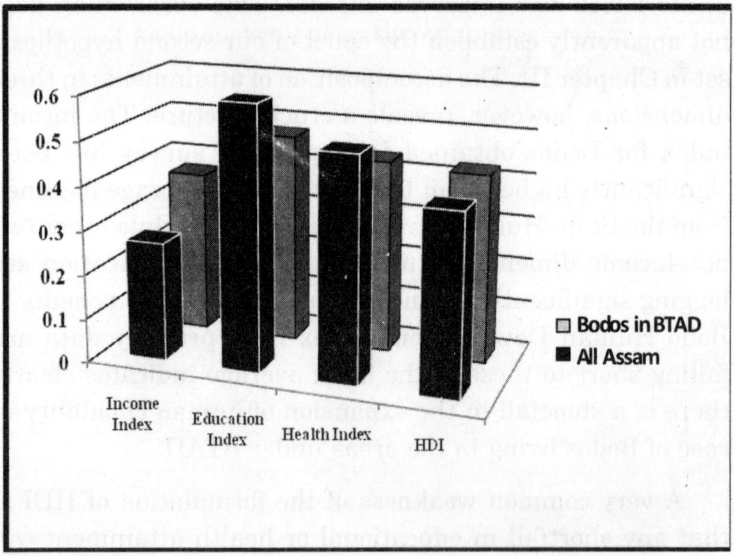

Fig. 5.1: Status of Human Development in Assam: A Comparison

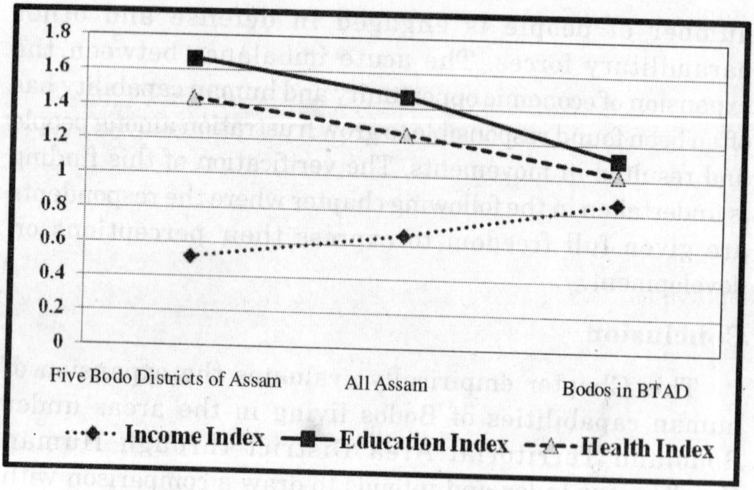

Fig. 5.2: Relative Contribution to Overall Expansion of Human Capability

Source: Elaboration based on Assam Human Development Report 2003; Human development of Bodos-2003

The figure indicates clearly that for the Bodos the relative contribution of income is much higher as compared to the state average as well as the average of the five Bodo Districts of Assam. In other two cases the non-income components of Human Development Index contributes more to that of income component while in case of Bodos as obtained from primary observation the income component dominates the non-income components. The Non-Income Human Development Index as from primary data for Bodos is merely 83 per cent of State average in 2003, and about 90 per cent of five districts' average. At the other end, Income Index for Bodos is about 137 per cent higher than the State average, over 200 per cent higher than five Bodo Districts' average. This observation is significant in the sense that there is a sharp contrast in the expansions of economic opportunities and human capabilities in case of Bodos. The achievement in human development of Bodos is merely income based as significant

number of people is engaged in defense and other paramilitary forces. The acute imbalance between the expansion of economic opportunity and human capability has often been found responsible to grow frustration among people and resulted in movements. The verification of this finding is undertaken in the following chapter where the respondents are given full freedom to express their perceptions on development.

Conclusion

This Chapter empirically evaluates the expansion of human capabilities of Bodos living in the areas under Bodoland Territorial Area District through Human Development Index and intends to draw a comparison with that of the state of Assam. It is observed that Bodos are lagging marginally behind the rest of the state in over all expansion of capabilities. However, the distinguishing feature of human development of Bodos has been comparatively income-driven as compared to the overall State scenario. The expansion of economic opportunity is found unaccomplished with parallel expansion human capabilities. This could be one of possible reasons of social unrest and frustration.

6

Bodo Aspirations and Expectation: Focus Group Discussion

This penultimate description attempts to capture qualitative judgments of Bodo people respondents about their developmental issues and social-cultural factors that have impact on their expectation and aspirations of their role in enhancing behaviour change. The study exists two folds, first it sought to establish opinion evaluation in terms of development and second one is an empirical study using data collection methods of Focus Group Discussions and key informant interviews to establish the extent to which Bodo aspiration and expectations with social cultural factors contribute to Bodo movement. The study was designed carried out in four districts of BTAD. Social and cultural factors were said to have significant impact on developmental related issue. Traditional belief and religious gatherings activities, language, cultural, custom, marriage ceremony etc. were reported to be the main social factors which impact on social change and ceremonies as well as funeral rites and traditional rituals were some of the cultural factors which may also influence in enhancing people's aspiration and expectations.

However, at this stage of the study we recall the fact that common respondents are not aware of human development as a concept, nor about the mathematics involved in measuring it. To let the respondents express their priorities and better understand their well-beings we organize *focus group discussions* (FGD) on developmental issues. A cordial atmosphere was created during the discussions where the respondents were first individually requested to respond to few major questions on unity and peace lovingness nature of Bodo Community, urgency of their call for restoration of peace, poor governance and their impact on illfare, etc and then they were absolutely free to express their views during discussion on on-going Bodo movements, and about the expected outcomes of the movement. Our interest was solely focused on what the people think they should be able to do and be in their potential functioning and capabilities.

Focus Group Discussion: Methodological Basics

The Focus Group Discussion (FGD) is a powerful qualitative method, generally applied in social science researches, to obtain in-depth information on concepts, perceptions and ideas of a group on social, economic, political issues that directly or indirectly shape their lives [Asiimwe et. al. (2003)]. It refers to the group discussion participated by certain number of persons guided by a facilitator, during which group members talk freely and spontaneously on certain topic(s). Hence, the method aims to be more effective and authentic than the common *question-answer-type* interactions. The underlying ideas behind this qualitative technique traces upon the fact that group members discuss the topic among themselves in a cordial atmosphere where the group members feel absolutely free from any kind of pressure from social, political, administrative or religious angles. The FGD can effectively explore perceptions of the participants even on controversial topics. However, proceedings of Focus Group Discussion has been interactive in nature, each discussion builds on the previous one with elaborated or better focused set of things for discussion. The technique is regarded as a powerful research tool which can provide valuable spontaneous information in a short period of time. However, it is suggested that the information gathered through FGD should not be used for typical quantitative purposes such as testing of hypothesis or the generalization of things for larger areas.

The primary requirement for conducting an effective discussion points towards thorough knowledge of local conditions. The members selected for the discussion may not necessarily be homogenous. Their opinions are likely to differ according to their gender, educational attainments, political affiliations, economic status, and ethnic as well as religious identity. These differences are likely to be reflected on the perceptions of the problems they regularly suffer from, and dream for possible solutions. The primary quality of the researchers conducting group discussion requires, therefore, complete awareness of these differences.

Selected members should preferably be of the same socio-economic and ethno-political background or have a similar connection in relation to the issues under investigation. At the same time the facilitator is expected to speak in the language/dialect of the participants. There should be a precise list of topics to be covered during the session in the mind of the facilitator so that all relevant topics are discussed, no item is left. It is highly recommended that the entire discussion should be recorded in a suitable electronic machine so that the facilitator can play the role of a facilitator solely, and remains free from the act of repertoire. It is suggested that in no circumstances facilitator should control the direction of the discussion. In the situation when some of the participants are using words which are *un-parliamentarian* or abusive in nature the facilitator is expected not to stop the member directly as it may spoil the entire proceedings.

Organization of Groups

Considering the relevant basics for conducting effective focus group discussion, elaborated in the previous section, we have organized twelve group discussions in each of our study villages. As opinions on expectations as well as aspirations vary significantly across the age and sex of the people we make some broad grouping of the respondents covering all these aspects of human welfare. The focus group discussions were conducted with a total number of 120 respondents, taking 10 respondents from each of our sample villages. The characteristics of total respondents participated in all twelve *focus discussions* are designed with the following number of participants.

Table 6.1
Respondents' characteristics

Age-Group	*Male*	*Female*	*Total*
20-35	27	19	46
36-50	29	21	50
Above 50	11	13	24
Grand Total	67	53	120

In order to ensure ethnic representativeness, the study has been divided into three ages of groupings which are internally fairly homogeneous in terms of their social and cultural characteristics. These three ages of groupings include twenty to thirty five, thirty six to fifty and above fifty. However, to maintain a certain degree of homogeneity among the participants in terms of their age and sex in four villages the groups were formed with exclusive male participants, in another four villages only female participants. In remaining four villages groups were of mixed participants in which age-groups were taken as criterion of forming the groups. The groups in the villages namely, Koklabari, Khathalguri, Hazira and Aidhuli were exclusively of male participants, while in the villages namely, Kharua, Axiguri, Bamunkhata and Patgaon were of exclusively of female participants. In the remaining villages namely, Dangaigaon, Dotama, Bahmolla and Galasuba groups were formed with mixed participants. Moreover, the groups with exclusive male participants were also classified according to the age of the respondents. In first three villages the respondents were invited from similar age-group: groups in Koklabari, Khathalguri, Hazira villages were formed with twenty to thirty five, thirty six to fifty and above fifty male participants respectively. However, in Aidhuli a mixed group with exclusive male participants was formed. Table: 6.2 depicts the composition of respondents in these four villages with exclusive male participants. Similarly, the groups in Kharua, Axiguri and Bamunkhata villages were formed with twenty to thirty five, thirty six to fifty and above fifty female participants respectively while the group in Patgaon village was a mixture of all age-group female participants. This type of age grouping is designed to carry out opinions of Bodo people on developmental issue and aspiration and expectations from development discourse. And also to know categorically their qualitative judgments regarding development and socio-cultural factors which contribute on their behavioral change of mind. In each of the selected groups, 53 female were randomly selected in which three Focus Group Discussions were held in each village and 67 male were selected in which three Focus Group Discussion were held in each village. A total of one hundred twenty participants for Focus Group Discussions were conducted in the four districts taking 30 participants from each district.

Table 6.2
Focus group discussions with exclusively male participants

Formation of group: Koklabari (Jalah) Baksa			
Age-Group	*Male*	*Female*	*Total*
20-35	10	-	10
36-50	-	-	-
Above 50	-	-	-
Grand Total	10	-	10
Formation of group: Khathalguri (Udalguri) Udalguri			
Age-Group	*Male*	*Female*	*Total*
20-35	-	-	-
36-50	10	-	10
Above 50	-	-	-
Grand Total	10	-	10
Formation of group: Hazira (Mosalpur) Baksa			
Age-Group	*Male*	*Female*	*Total*
20-35	-	-	-
36-50	-	-	-
Above 50	10	-	10
Grand Total	10	-	10
Formation of group: Aidhuli (Sidli) Chirang			
Age-Group	*Male*	*Female*	*Total*
20-35	3	-	3
36-50	6	-	6
Above 50	1	-	1
Grand Total	10	-	10

Table: 6.3 depicts the composition of respondents in these four villages with exclusive female participants.

Table 6.3
Focus group discussions with exclusively female participants

Formation of group: Kharua (Barama) Baksa			
Age-Group	*Male*	*Female*	*Total*
20-35	-	10	10
36-50	-	-	-
Above 50	-	-	-
Grand Total	-	10	10

Formation of group: Axiguri (Borobazar) Chirang			
Age-Group	*Male*	*Female*	*Total*
20-35	-	-	-
36-50	-	10	10
Above 50	-	-	-
Grand Total	-	10	10

Formation of group: Bamuhkhata (Gosaigaon) Kokrajhar			
Age-Group	*Male*	*Female*	*Total*
20-35	-	-	-
36-50	-	-	-
Above 50	-	10	10
Grand Total	-	10	10

Formation of group: Patgaon (Titaguri) Kokrajhar			
Age-Group	*Male*	*Female*	*Total*
20-35	-	3	3
36-50	-	4	4
Above 50	-	3	3
Grand Total	-	10	10

Table 6.4
Focus group discussions with mixed participants

Formation of group: Dangaigaon (Manigpur) Chirang

Age-Group	*Male*	*Female*	*Total*
20-35	6	4	10
36-50	-	-	-
Above 50	-	-	-
Grand Total	6	4	10

Formation of group: Dotama (Dotama) Kokrajhar

Age-Group	*Male*	*Female*	*Total*
20-35	-	-	-
36-50	7	3	10
Above 50	-	-	-
Grand Total	7	3	10

Formation of group: Bahmolla (Koirabari) Udalguri

Age-Group	*Male*	*Female*	*Total*
20-35	5	2	7
36-50	2	1	3
Above 50	-	-	-
Grand Total	7	3	10

Formation of group: Galasuba (Bhergaon) Udalguri

Age-Group	*Male*	*Female*	*Total*
20-35	3	-	3
36-50	4	3	7
Above 50	-	-	-
Grand Total	7	3	10

We have mentioned earlier that in remaining four villages, namely Dangaigaon, Dotama, Bahmolla and Galasuba, the groups were formed with both male and female participants. Table: 6.4 depicts the composition of respondents in these four villages with both male and female participants. In first two villages of this category age-groups of the respondents were considered for their selection: the composition of focus group discussion in Dangaigaon village contained participants exclusively from the age-group *20-35* of both sexes, while in Dotama village all participants were selected from the age-group *36-50*. The groups in other two villages, namely Bahmolla and Galasuba, were in fact arbitrary combinations of all age-groups and both sexes.

Findings of Focus Group Discussion

This section summarizes the findings on Bodo community perception of development and key factors that are treated as crucial for their persistent backwardness in developmental matters. Participants in focus group discussions were asked to prioritize what they perceived to be major advantages and obstacles to change the scenario in future i.e. the key factors that according to the participants push them behind. Focus Group Discussions were conducted in twelve study villages with purposively selected groups of participants of different age-groups and sexes. Given the fact that the respondents are not aware of human development as concept, nor about the mathematics involved in measuring human development the proceedings of discussions were solely on non-technical language. We let respondents establish what most important and relevant for themselves without any interference or suggestions.

The discussion focused first of all the key advantages of Bodo community that can be considered as major resources to achieve their perceived goal of development. The unity and the peace-loving feature of Bodo community have been perceived as the major resources, while hard-working skills, brotherly feelings for non-Bodo tribal population as well as for the non-tribal communities living around emerge as next important resources. Few participants, however, emphasizes on tribal values of the community as a whole. About 40 per cent of the total participants across the age groups of both sexes reported that they consider the unity of Bodo community is the major advantage for achieving developmental goals. Nearly 27 per cent participants consider the peace-loving feature of the community should be treated as most important resource.

The second topic of discussion focused on the major obstacles that came in the way of development as potential barriers. In this particular topic participants mentioned different aspects for their overall *illfare*.

About 73 per cent of male respondents blame poor governance responsible for their overall *illfare* while 63 per cent women feel that for their betterment immediate solution of Bodo agitation as well as the restoration of peace is necessary. Lack of educational infrastructure and poor educational services are pointed out by the young respondents of both sexes. Health services are also found inadequate. Ethnic identity plays a crucial role in the mind of the older respondents. About Bodo movement, surprisingly, there is hardly any support for the violence; however, the opinion is clearly divided on the issue of separate Bodo State as the solution of the problem. An acute feeling of exclusion in political as well as developmental decision-making programs is reflected clearly during the sessions of *focus group discussions*. The other dominant factor behind the mounting frustration among the respondents has been revealed during the course of focus group discussion as the attainment of statehood by small tribal groups in the neighboring areas in the north-eastern region.

Conclusion

This Chapter intends to capture the perception of the respondents on development and on the decades old agitation for full-fledged statehood for the Bodos in Assam. The discussions reveal that the issue is a complex one and many factors had led the feelings of exclusion in the mind of Bodos. Poor expansion of human capabilities due to miserable public services and rampant corruption along with ethnicity-led identity crises triggered the frustration and feeling of exclusion in the mind of common people.

7

Summary and Conclusion

As is obvious here a review of the key findings of the present research is given and certain policy measures are suggested. It also points out the limitations that remained in the present study and provides a broad view of the future researches in the relevant fields.

The present research was carried out in three major steps: first was a *document review step* where we presented a detailed assessment of the expansion of human capabilities from the existing secondary information available in various government publications. In this step we compared the status of human development indicators in five Bodo inhabited districts of Assam and that of the rest of the state. Second was the *question-answer type Interview step* in which stage an empirical study intended to generate information on overall expansion of human capability and its decomposition over attainments. Following standard methodology of Human Development Index (HDI) we evaluate empirically the level of human development of Bodos living in the areas under BTAD. This step of the research was carried out on the basis of primary information collected from randomly selected villages of all the four districts under BTAD. The final step conducts *Focus Group Discussions (FGD)* to obtain qualitative judgments of the concerned people of different categories. This stage of the study intended to gather the perception of the common people on their development and aspirations. The decision of the hypotheses that were set in Chapter III has been taken on the basis of the results obtained in three stages of our research. Here we present a step-wise review of the findings, and attempt to interpret them in the context of our hypotheses.

The document review stage of the present study examined the stock of secondary information to evaluate the status of Bodo inhabited districts in terms of human development indicators. Despite the fact that Assam is a poor performer in the country the Bodo-inhabited districts of our concern are lagging significantly behind in some aspects of development as compared to the state average. This observation, however, is not sufficient enough to draw any inference on the first hypothesis of the study such that the poor performance in human development triggered the on-going movement for the protection of ethnic identity and thereby overall development. The second stage of our research i.e., the *question-answer type step* establishes the fact clearly that Bodos are lagging marginally behind the rest of the state in overall expansion of human capabilities. After the findings obtained in this stage there remains no problem to accept the first hypothesis. In addition, the distinguishing feature of human development of Bodos, revealed in this stage of the study, indicates that it has been income-driven as compared to the overall State scenario. The expansion of economic opportunity remained unaccomplished with parallel expansion of human capabilities. This emerged as one of possible reasons of social unrest and frustration. At this stage of the study we accept the second hypothesis, set in the Chapter-III, saying that poor expansion of human capability played a crucial role in triggering of the movement. The decision of accepting two consecutive hypotheses of our study has been ratified ultimately in the final stage of the research.

The third as well as the final stage of the study which conducted *focused group discussions* in each of the study villages intended to capture the perception of the respondents on development; and also on the decades-old agitation for full-fledged statehood for the Bodos in Assam. This stage of the study endorses both of the hypotheses set initially. The discussions moreover reveal that the issue of identity and feeling of exclusion had also played critical role in the mind of Bodos. Poor expansion of human capabilities due to miserable public services and rampant corruption along with ethnicity-led identity crises triggered the frustration, and spread the feeling of exclusion in the mind of common people.

Policy Recommendations

The findings of this study have important policy implications. Understanding various factors leading to political economy of Bodo movement in the state has been crucial for formulating effective policies. The policy suggestions arising out of the present study indicates for evolving an inclusive policy model for development where all sections of the population feel included. Everybody should have equal role in the decision-making of the matters that often shape their lives. There should be equal respect to all and marginal people should be respected. Economic prosperity does not guaranteed human development. Human development is increasingly viewed as the ultimate objective of development in place of Economic Growth. Links between human development and economic growth remain of critical importance since economic growth appears to be a foremost contributor to sustained progress in human development. Moreover improvements in human development are not only the fundamental development goal, but human development is itself an important contributor to economic prosperity or economic growth over time. Clearly, there exist strong connections between economic growth and human development. On the one hand, economic growth provides the resources to permit sustained improvements in human development. On the other, human development improvements raise the capacities of economic agents who make the critical contribution to economic growth or economic prosperity. Each of these relationships has often been acknowledged separately, for example, the way economic growth or economic prosperity affects human development forms part of the basic needs literature, while the impact of improved labour quality of economic growth has been widely explored in the human capital literature. All high income groups of family can not enjoy full of peace and freedom and get welfare, so emphasis should be shifted from income approach to human development approach in which income acts as means only to an end. An unprecedented effort would be required to bring back the lost faith in the mind of common pcoplc. Pcople of all spheres of life should work together to achieve this goal.

Limitations

Despite a significant contribution in the literature of human development and identity issues the present study suffers from few limitations. Due to severe scarcity of secondary data on Bodo population the study was based on collected primary information exclusively from the Bodo population living in the areas under BTAD. On the basis of which the Human Development Index (HDI) for the Bodo community was computed. Along with this, the information of the Non-Bodo population living in the same region would have given much better scope of comparison between two communities.

Future Scope

The present research is a preliminary study of a particular ethnic group that suffers from acute feelings of exclusion for over a century and agitating for the establishment of their role in decision-making. The evolution of the process through which simple identity issues turned into massive violence has been studied under the broadest possible doctrine of capability-based development thinking. The topic is not only relevant in national context where thousands of ethnic groups are in the same row, the issue is equally important in global perspective. A number of studies can be undertaken by the future scholars following the framework developed in the present research. The important contribution of the present study is the observation that the acute imbalance between the expansion of economic opportunity and enhancement of human capability were one of the major factors behind the political-ethnic unrest in the region. This particular angle of observation can be taken as a solid basis of many future social science researches.

Select Bibliography

ABSU (1987): *Why Separate State of Bodoland: Demand and Justifications*, Kokrajhar, Assam.

Adam, C. and S. Dercon (2009): "The Political Economy of Development: An Assessment", *Oxford Review of Economic Policy*, Vol-25 No.2, pp.173-189.

Anand, S. and A. Sen (1997): "Concepts of Human Development and Poverty: A Multidimensional Perspective", Human Development Report 1997 Paper: *Human Poverty,* UNDP, New York.

Anand, S. and A. Sen (1997): *Human Development Report 1997,* Oxford University Press, New York, Technical Note 1 and Chapter 1.

Anand, S. and A. Sen (1999): *Human Development Report 1999,* Oxford University Press, New York, Panel of Consultants on Human Development Index Revision, Technical Note.

Anand, S. and A. Sen (1994): "Human Development Index: Methodology and Measurement", Occasional Paper 12, UNDP, Human Development Report Office, New York.

Anand, S. and A. Sen (1995): "Gender Inequality in Human Development: Theories and Measurement", Occasional Paper 19, UNDP, Human Development Report Office, New York.

Anderson, E.A. (1911): "Introduction" in Rev. S. Endle (ed.) *The Kacharis*, Delhi Cosmo Publication, Delhi.

Asiimwe, D, R. Kibombo and S. Neema (2003) *Focus Disscussion on Social Cultural Factors Impacting on HIV/AIDS in Uganda*. A Report for Ministry of Finance, Planning and Economic Development/UNDP. Kampala, Uganda. http://www.aidsuganda.org/pdf/social cultural factors. pdf

Bairathy, S. (1988): *Tribal Culture, Economy and Health*, Rawat Publications, New Delhi.

Barooah, D.P. (2004): "Reflections on India's North-East: Between Past and Future" in *Communal Harmony among Tribal and Non-Tribal Communities of North East India,* Published by Assam Institute of Research for Tribals and Scheduled Castes, Guwahati, Assam, pp.16-26.

Baruah, I., S. Sengupta, and D.D. Das (2002): *Ethnic Groups Continuities and Social Change in North East India*, Mittal Publications, New Delhi.

Basumatary, B.K. (1992): "Political Aspiration of the Aboriginal Primitive Tribes vis-à-vis the United Tribal Nationalists Liberation Front" in L.S. Gassah (ed.) *Regional Political Parties in North-East India*, Omson Publication, New Delhi, pp. 88-95.

Basumatary, S.C. (1993): *Bibar*, Bodo Employee Literary Organization, Kokrajhar, Assam, Vol-2, First Edition.

Basumatary, S.C. (1994): *The Baksa,* Ludra Press, Moshalpur, Assam.

Basumatary, Z.D. (ed.) (2002): *Sonathi Khampha*, A Souvenir of *Bodo Sahitya Sabha*, Kokrajhar, Assam.

Basumatary, S. (2005): *The Bodo*, Bodo Sahitya Sabha, 45th Issue, Koklabari, Assam.

Beteille, A. (1992): *Society and Politics in India: Essays in a Comparative Perspective*, Oxford University Press, Delhi, pp. 57-78.

Bhagabati, A.C. (1992): *Tribal Transformation in Assam and Northeast India: An Appraisal of Emerging Ideological Dimensions*, Inter-India Publications, New Delhi, pp. 487-509.

Bhagabati, A.C. (2002): "Ethnic Identities in North-East India" N.K. Bose Memorial Lectures, Vihangama, *IGNCA News Letter*, Vol-2, March.

Bhattacharjee, C. (1996): *Ethnicity and Autonomy Movement*, Vikash Publishing House, Delhi.

Bhattacharya, H. (1969): *The Cultural Heritage of India,* Ramkrishna Mission Institute of Culture, Calcutta.

Biggeri, M., Liibanora, R., Mariani, S.L. Menchini, L. (2006): Children Conceptualising their capabilities; results of a survey conducted during the first children's world congress on child labour, journal of Human Development,Vol-7, No.1 59-83.

Bhuyan, S.K. (ed.) (1951): *The Kachari Burunji*, Department of Historical and Antiquarian Studies, Guwahati, Assam.

Bora, R. (1990): "The Contribution of Bodo People in Assamese Culture" in *Chaithi* (A Souvenir of Bodo Sahitya Sabha), Dhekiajuli, Assam.

Bordoloi, B.N. (1984): *The Dimasa-Kachari of Assam: A Brief Introduction*, Tribal Research Institute, Guwahati, Assam, p. 6.

Bordoloi, B.N. (1984): "Some Aspects of Etymology of the Term Dimasa-Kachari" in S. Karotemprel (ed.) *The Tribes of North East India*, Firma KLM Pvt. Ltd., First edition, Calcutta, p.245.

Bordoloi, S. (2004): "Ongoing Violence and Repercussions", *Communal Harmony among Tribal and Non-Tribal Communities of North East India,* Published by Assam Institute of Research for Tribals and Scheduled Castes, Guwahati, Assam, pp.119-133.

Boro, A. (1994): "The Rise of the Bodo Middle Class- Its Impact on Literature, Culture and Society of the Bodos", *The Bodo* (A Souvenir of Bodo Sahitya Sabha), 19th Issue, Guwahati, Assam, pp.11-18.

Boro, B.D. (1985): *History of Boro Literature in Songai*, A Souvenir of Bodo Sahitya Sabha, Kokrajhar, Assam, pp. 43-44.

Boro, T. (1993): *The Bodo,* Bodo Sahitya Sabha, Issue 40, Guwahati, Assam.

Bose, J. K. (1980): *Glimpses of Tribal Life in North-East India*, Institute of Social Research and Applied Anthropology, Calcutta.

Brahma C.S. (1986): "On Udayachal Movement", *Recent Trends in Political Development of the North-East*, A Monograph of the Department of Political Science, Diphu Govt. College, Diphu, Assam, Vol.1, p.12.

Brahma, K. (1983): "Gods and Goddesses of the Bodos: How they Worshipped", *Journal of North East India Council for Social Science Research*, Issue 7, pp. 35-38.

Brahma, K. (1989): *Aspects of Social Customs of the Boros*, Spectrum Publication, Kokrajhar, Assam.

Brahma, K. (1992): *A Study of Socio-Religious Beliefs, Practices of Ceremonies*, Punthi Pusttak, Calcutta.

Brahma, K. (1998): *A Study in Cultural Heritage of the Boros*, Spectrum Publication, Kokrajhar, Assam.

Brahma, M.M. (1983): "The Bodo-Kacharis of Assam- A Brief Introduction", *Bulletin of the Tribal Research Institute*, Guwahati, Assam, Vol.1, No.1, p.34 & 52.

Brahma, Y.Z. (2001): *Bodoland Movement: A Dream and Reality*, Published by the All Bodo Students Union, Kokrajhar, Assam.

Chatterjee, S.K. (1974): *Kirata-Jana-Kriti, the Indo-Mongolois, their Contribution to the History and Culture of India*, The Asiatic Society of Bengal, Calcutta, pp. 45-46.

Chottopadhyay, D.K. (1990): *History of the Assamese Movement since 1947*, Minerva Associate Publication Pvt. Ltd., Calcutta.

Comin, F. and Teschel (2006): "Introduction: Capabilities and Identity", *Journal of Economic Methodology*, Vol-13 No.3, pp. 293-298.

Daimary, B. (1987): "The Boro", *Proceedings of North East India History Association* (NEIHA), Eighth Session, Kokrajhar, Assam, pp. 529-530.

Daimary, B. (1986): *Boro-Politics in Assam since Independence*, Unpublished Ph. D Dissertation, Department of History, School of Social Sciences, NEHU, Shillong.

Das, B.M. (1984): "Physical Anthropology of the Tribes of North East India" in S. Karotemprel (ed.) *The Tribes of North-East India*, Firma KLM Pvt. Ltd., Calcutta, p.44.

Das, J.N. (1989): "Udayachal Movement in Assam- A Case of Socio-Political Identity for the Bodos", *The Indian Journal of Political Science*, Indian Political Science Association, Madras, Vol.50, No. 3, July-Sept, p. 335.

Das, S.T. (1986): "Kachari People", *Tribal Life of North-Eastern India*, Gyan Publishing House, Delhi, p.263

Das, S.T. (1993): *Tribal Development and Socio-Cultural Matrix*, Krishna Publications, Delhi.

Endle, S. (2011): *The Kacharis*, Akansha Publishing House, New Delhi.

Fukuda-Parr, S. (2004): "Cultural Freedom and Human Development Today", *Daedalus,* Vol.133, p.133. <http://www.questia.com/googleScholar.qst;jsessionid=LVkZh92MCJrzXCGTsF9Xpvcp0FyjTdy2h5QTNQNHWVFpFH6vZyN2!157216685! 1154483301? docId=5007154734> (visited on 12-01-2007)

Gait, E.A. (1984): *A History of Assam*, LBS Publication, Gauhati, Assam, pp. 247-248

Gierson, G.A. (1903): *The Linguistic Survey of India*, New Delhi, Vol.3, Part-I &II.

Gohain, H. (1989): "Bodo Stir in Perceptive", *Economic and Political Weekly*, Vol-24 No.25, June 24, pp. 1377-1379.

Goswami, M.C. (1971): *Tribe-Peasant-Caste Relations in North East India*, Fifty Eight Annual Session of Indian Science Congress, Bangalore.

G.O.I. (2002): *National Human Development Report 2001*, Planning Commission, OUP, New Delhi.

Gupta, B.N. (1989): "Bodo Agitation- Problem and Prospects", *Mainstream*, June 24, Vol.7, No.39, New Delhi.

Hutchinson, J. and Smith, A.D. (ed.) (1996): *Ethnicity,* Oxford University Press, New York.

Karotemprel, S. (ed.) (1984): *The Tribes of North-East*, Firma KLM Pvt. Ltd., Calcutta.

Khungkhra, S. (1982): *An Introduction of the Mishing and the Bodos*, Spectrum Publication, Kokrajhar, Assam.

Lahary, M.R. (1984): "Early History of Bodo", *The Bodo,* A Souvenir of Bodo Sahitya Sabha, Kokrajhar, Assam, pp.1-2.

Mukhajee, S.K. (1984): *Socio-Political Movement of the Bodo-Kacharis and its Impact*, Social Science Study Centre, Shillong, Meghalaya, p. 11.

Mushahary, R.N. (1987): "Traditional Religion of the Boro of Assam", *Proceeding of North East India History Association,* Eighth Session, Kohima, Nagaland, pp. 510-511.

Narzinari, H. (2000): *Re-assertiveness of the Great Boros*, Published by David Iswarary, Calcutta.

Nath, M.K. (2003): "Bodo Insurgency in Assam: New Accord and New Problem", *Strategic Analysis*, Vol-27 No.4, pp.533-544.

Nath, R.N. (1978): *The Background of Assamese Culture*, Spectrum Publications, Guwahati, pp.15-16.

Nayak, P. and Thomas, E.D. (2007): *Human Development & Deprivation in Meghalaya,* Akansha Publishing House, New Delhi, India.

NCAER (2004): *East India Human Development Report*, Oxford University Press, New Delhi.

Nibedon, N. (1981): *North East India: The Ethnic Explosion*, Lancers Publishers, New Delhi.

Nurse, K. (2007): "Culture and Human Development", A Policy Discussion Paper- Common Wealth People's Forum: Realizing People's Potential. <http://www.commonwealthfoundation.com/uploads/documents/Culture%20Discussion%20Paper%20Nurse.pdf> (visited on 12-01-2007)

Pulloppillil, T. and A.J. Luckal (1997): *The Boros: Children Bhullumbutter*, Spectrum Publications, Guwahati, Assam.

Rastogi, P.N. (1986): *Ethnic Tensions in Indian Society*, Mittal Publications, Delhi.

Ray, S. (2009): *Dynamic Links between Economy and Human Development: A study of Indian States.* Awarded Ph. D. Thesis submitted to North Eastern Hill University, Shillong.

Ray, S. (2010): Transformation of Economic Growth into Human Development: A Long Term Study of Indian States in Nayak P.(eds.) *Economic Growth and Human Development in North East India,* Oxford University Press, New Delhi.

Roy Burman, B.K. (1994): *Tribes in Perspective*, Mittal Publications, New Delhi.

Roy, A. (1995): *The Boro Imbroglio*, Spectrum Publications, Guwahati, Assam.

Rout, H.S. and Panda, P.K. (ed.) (2009): *Human Development Dimension and Strategies,* New Century Publications, New Delhi.

Sen, A. (1979): "Informational Analysis of Moral Principles", in Ross Harrison (ed.) *Rational Action: Studies in Philosophy and Social Science,* Cambridge University Press, Cambridge.

Sen, A. (1977): "Rational Fools: A Critique of the Behavioral Foundations of Economic Theory", *Philosophy and Public Affairs*, Vol-6 No.3, pp.317-344.

Sen, A. (1999): *Development as Freedom,* Oxford University Press, New York.

Sen, A. (2005): *The Argumentative Indian,* Penguin Books, London.

Sen, A. (2005$_a$): "Cultural Identity, Democracy and Global Equity", Keynote Address: Third Forum on Human Development, Paris, January 17, 2005. <http://hdr.undp.org/docs/events/global_forum/2005/speeches/Sen_keynote_eng.pdf> (visited on 12-01-2007)

Sen, A. (2006): *Identity and Violence: The Illusion of Destiny*, Penguin Books, London.

Singh, G. (2004): "Social Change in Tribal Society and the Role of Non-Tribal Groups towards Change: A Study on Major Groups of South Kamrup and Goalapara District in Assam", *Communal Harmony among Tribal and Non-Tribal Communities of North East India,* Published by Assam Institute of Research for Tribals and Scheduled Castes, Guwahati, Assam, pp.140-145.

Soppit, C.A. (1885): *A Historical and Descriptive Account of the Kachari Tribe in the N.C. Hills with Specimens of Tales and Folklore*, Shillong, Meghalaya.

Srinivas, M.N. (1962): *Caste in Modern India and Other Essays*, Asia Publishing House, Bombay.

Thakur, P. (1982): *India's North-East: Multi-Faceted View*, Prakash Publishing House, Tinsukia, Assam.

UNDP (2007): *Measuring Human Development: A Primer*. Guidelines and Tools for Statistical Research, Analysis and Advocacy. <http://hdr.undp.org/en/media/primer_complete.pdf> (visited on 24-11-2008).

Index